Christi Carter's Art of ACCESSORIZING

FOUR SIMPLE ELEMENTS THAT BRING YOUR HOME TO LIFE

MEREDITH® BOOKS

DES MOINES, IOWA

Christi Carter's Art of Accessorizing

Editor: Vicki Leigh Ingham
Contributing Editors: Amber Barz, Karin Baji Holms, Heidi T. King, Donna Talley
Graphic Designers: Andrea Quam, Design Group Inc., and Ray Neubauer
Copy Chief: Terri Fredrickson
Publishing Operations Manager: Karen Schirm
Edit and Design Production Coordinator: Mary Lee Gavin
Book Production Managers: Pam Kvitne, Marjorie J. Schenkelberg, Rick von Holdt, Mark Weaver
Contributing Copy Editor: Jane Woychick
Contributing Proofreaders: Beth Havey, Margaret Smith, Jody Speer
Contributing Photographers: Michael Partenio, Dan Piassick, Scott Sloan
Contributing Photostylist: Mary Baskin, Marlene Dibrell, Joetta Moulden
Indexer: Stephanie Reymann
Editorial Assistant: Kaye Chabot
Cover Photograph: Dan Piassick

Meredith₀ Books

Editor in Chief: Linda Raglan Cunningham
Design Director: Matt Strelecki
Managing Editor: Gregory H. Kayko
Executive Editor: Denise L. Caringer

Publisher: James D. Blume
Executive Director, Marketing: Jeffrey Myers
Executive Director, New Business Development: Todd M. Davis
Executive Director, Sales: Ken Zagor
Director, Operations: George A. Susral
Director, Production: Douglas M. Johnston
Business Director: Jim Leonard

Vice President and General Manager: Douglas J. Guendel

Meredith Publishing Group

President: Jack Griffin
Senior Vice President: Bob Mate

Meredith Corporation

Chairman and Chief Executive Officer: William T. Kerr
President and Chief Operating Officer: Stephen M. Lacy

In Memoriam: E. T. Meredith III (1933–2003)

All of us at Meredith₀ Books are dedicated to providing you with information and ideas to enhance your home. We welcome your comments and suggestions. Write to us at: Meredith Books, Home Decorating and Design Editorial Department, 1716 Locust St., Des Moines, IA 50309-3023.

If you would like to purchase any of our home decorating and design, cooking, crafts, gardening, or home improvement books, check wherever quality books are sold. Or visit us at: meredithbooks.com

Table of Contents

I grew up surrounded by wise and inventive women—women who knew that the power of accessories went far beyond just completing a look. The women in my family were well aware that the smallest of touches can create an exciting uniqueness, enabling one to be herself. The brooch that becomes a conversation-starter, a stunning new pair of shoes that make a woman want to dance all her cares away, a whimsical handbag that hints at the wearer's sly wit—these make statements that convey a person's inner self and spark.

For a home, key accessories work the same way. Imaginatively designed accessories as well as treasured heirlooms add a keen aesthetic to a room and project a distinctive personality—yours.

For me, accessories have an even greater significance. My grandmother, Mary Crowley, believed that the home is the greatest influence on human character and she made a career out of teaching women how to use accessories to enliven a room. She founded a company called Home Interiors & Gifts—today the world's largest direct seller of home decorative accessories. Mary Crowley has changed the lives of hundreds of thousands of women by enabling them to create lucrative businesses of their own by bringing beauty to one home at a time.

Her passion for home was infectious. Even as a little girl, I remember how she and my mother set the scene for our family gatherings with a beautiful table filled with flowers and illuminating candlelight. Mary Crowley transformed the most ordinary events into extraordinary ones with her attention to the special details. Now that I have my own family, I share that dream of designing a space where we can gather and build new memories, a haven where my family loves to spend time.

This book's aim is to help you create a haven where *your* family will love to spend time. While there are numerous books on decorating, none focus on what to do after you've picked a style and arranged the furniture. Yet in decor, accessories are those special pieces that stamp your signature on your home. They reflect the objects about which you are most passionate and which reflect your unique sensibility in accessorizing. Here is where the fun begins!

Over the years, I have turned the lessons learned from my grandmother into a simple decorating strategy by breaking down accessorizing into four distinct but simple elements—wall decor, signature accessories, flowers and foliage, and ambience. On the following pages, you'll discover hundreds of beautiful photos, accessorizing tips, and words of experience to help you build your confidence and your own identity. You'll learn how to express your own style through accessories and discover how to give your home a new look—without investing in a whole new room!

The Art of Accessorizing is a tribute to my grandmother and to women everywhere who share her desire to make a haven for the ones they love. My grandmother left another rich legacy – the art of giving to others. Home Interiors Charitable Foundation, supported by the thousands of talented women her company today empowers, funds many worthy causes. And now you will have a hand in that altruism too—any profits I receive from the sale of this book will be donated to support the Women Build initiative of Habitat for Humanity. This wonderful program allows women everywhere to cherish a home in which they can express their own dreams of creating a haven for their families.

Enjoy!

Christi Carter-Urschel

The dining room where your family and friends gather to dine and enjoy close company should emanate warmth and hospitality. The floral arrangements on the table (above) are in contemporary glass containers to tone down the formality of the room. The bouquets stay below eye level to encourage conversation. An asymmetrical arrangement on the mantel also lessens the room's formal look and gives a welcoming atmosphere. I love to use place cards when entertaining, following my grandmother's lesson that place cards convey to guests, "I planned a place just for you."

The four step process to
PERSONAL STYLE

Accessories represent a powerful tool for making your home look and feel warm and inviting. To use accessories effectively, think of them as belonging to one of four categories that also represent steps in a process; working with one category at a time allows you to approach decorating a room in an easy, step-by-step, organized way that's both fun and creative.

First, start with the walls. Walls define the room's space; they're the shell you cover with color and fill with furniture. Dressing the walls with accessories animates the room, defines its character, and gives it focus. You have a wide array to choose from—framed art, plates or platters, textiles, wall vases, and even baskets can bring color, texture, and dimension to your walls. One point I keep in mind in my own home is to make sure the wall art is in proportion to the space I want to fill. In my kitchen, for example, I stacked two paintings on the wall between the antique hutch and the built-in bookshelves *(opposite)* because that space needed a strong statement to balance the visual weight of the hutch. I also use the area between the bookshelves for wall display—and I like to use items in unexpected ways. A painted tray *(right)* hangs as if it were a picture, while a cathedral-style candle sconce simply leans against the wall.

Doing the unexpected brings creativity to decorating: Treat the back of bookshelves as wall space (above) and hang a painted tray there instead of a framed print. Instead of laying a mesh basket flat, prop it up to provide a background for other objects. The dried flower arrangement repeats elements from the bouquet on the fireplace, creating a feeling of continuity.

Family pieces help tell your story. The small table between the armchairs (opposite) used to stand in my father's office; another memento from the past, the antique hutch was a gift from my parents. The polysilk greenery and the prominent vertical candlestick lamps soften the imposing lines of the hutch and pull the eye upward. The arrangement also balances the one on the fireplace and thus aids in unifying the room.

Collections can be the starting point for unusual wall displays as well as tabletop vignettes (above). To create an arrangement like this, imagine drawing a half-circle on the wall above the cabinet, then arranging the items on the wall to fill in that shape. The clocks and lamp on the cabinet top complete the shape. Additional accessories on the surface give depth and bring the display into the room.

I like to paint the back of bookshelves (opposite) *an accent color, usually a shade darker than the wall, to set off books and accessories. Bring the books to the front of the shelf instead of pushing them to the back. This placement creates a neater look and makes them feel more approachable, as if you were being invited to pull them out. For depth and interest, place greenery, collectibles, plates, or trays behind the books.*

The next step is to bring your personality into the room with signature accessories. Just as an autograph signifies the individual's name, so signature accessories embody your outlook on your living space and your individualistic "take" on your home as your family's haven.

Collections are important signature accessories because they reflect your past as well as the things you love. Arranging them into pleasing visual displays is a way of giving yourself engaging views that bring to mind happy memories. Our collection of clocks is an example. My husband and I began collecting clocks when we were first married, and the collection has continued to grow through gifts from family and friends. In our den, clocks are clustered on a side table and cabinet and play a starring role on the bookcase shelves. I've also arranged clock faces on the wall above the cabinet to create a secondary point of interest in this room. Clocks, books, and a lamp on the cabinet top create a foreground for the wall display. Notice how pieces overlap and a variety of shapes combine to encourage your eye to move from side to side as well as from front to back. Although what pleases your eye and expresses your taste is one important guideline, you'll find in Chapter 2 additional ideas for creating engaging displays on a variety of surfaces from coffee tables to sideboards and chests.

Signature accessories are the objects that help to tell a story—your story. Photographs are one of my favorite signature accessories because they so clearly tell people what you're about; they highlight the important experiences and the significant people in your life. My grandmother always kept a large bowl of current photographs on her kitchen island so everyone could see and enjoy them. In my home I maintain the tradition, placing loose photographs in a footed glass bowl on the chest in the family room *(right)*. Displaying special photos in charming picture frames adds color, shape and texture to tabletops and shelves and calls attention to your beloved photos.

Aside from photos, anything that delights your eye can become a signature accessory: everything from the more traditional decorative items such as figurines, vases, and art objects, to your uncommon treasures. For example, urns can be turned into umbrella stands, your grandmother's china gravy boats into pencil and pen holders and toast racks into letter holders. Use your imagination, have fun, and write your personal signature with decorative accessories instead of a pen!

The third step in accessorizing is to bring the room to life by introducing flowers and foliage. Flowers and plants enliven a room by bringing nature inside. Plants soften the hard lines

Filling a glass bowl with pictures rather than with potpourri or candles (above) adds a measure of surprise to the display on the chest. Just as sameness can be equated with dullness, so a dash of the unexpected can invigorate a room.

I felt the large painting above the mantel (opposite) seemed lost hanging by itself, so I added wall brackets filled with dried floral arrangements. Filling the metal brackets with faux pomegranates added color and visual weight. The mirrored wall on each side of the fireplace enhances the room's light and expands the sense of space. Mirrors make an eye-catching and unexpected background for the painting hung above the chest (opposite and above).

of shelves, tables, and architectural elements. Their twists and turns counterbalance stiff verticals and horizontals. Flowers, whether fresh, dried, or polysilk, bring color and a graceful flourish to tables and mantels. Plants and flowers need not be costly luxuries. If they come from your garden, they can point toward your creative way with growing things. Also, lovely but inexpensive foliage and flowers are sold at grocery stores. Living greenery and flowers make your room come alive, but also remember the benefits of polysilk florals, which closely resemble the look of real flowers and plants. With polysilk you can exercise your ingenuity by shaping the forms to look like living floral designs.

You don't need massive quantities of flowers to reap the benefits of their enlivening effect. In our family room just one tiny slipper orchid in a crystal bowl brings a sense of the garden to the coffee table. Fresh fruit falls into the flowers-and-foliage category as well. I love to keep a bowl of apples where they add color and fragrance, and people can feel free to take one.

Including fragrance is one part of the fourth step in the decorating process, creating ambience or mood. Ambience isn't just about how a room looks. It's about how it feels. It's about candlelight, soft accent lighting, pleasing scents, even music—all of the elements that help produce a welcoming, comfortable atmosphere. Perhaps because candlelight used to be reserved for special

occasions, it is one of the easiest, most effective ways to impart a mellow, inviting mood to the room. I always have candles burning in my house—I love the look, the fragrance, and the feeling they evoke in my home.

Lamplight is candlelight's cousin in instilling ambience. You need table lamps beside chairs and the sofa to provide light for reading, but those practical warm pools of light also make a room feel cheerful and cozy. On side tables, lamps also provide the backbone or anchor for arrangements of accessories and plants or flowers. On a side table in our den, for instance, the lamp is the tallest item on the table; its shade defines the boundaries for the display below—a framed photo, a glass globe, and flowers elevated on a book. This stable, balanced relationship between the shade and the items it shelters is comforting to the eye. Side tables are secondary focal points in the room, so make them a pleasing visual rest stop with a carefully arranged selection of functional and decorative items that express your interests and tastes.

Large-scale rooms call for large-scale furniture. To keep accessories from getting lost on a large coffee table, I group them on trays. I also use a fabric runner to add color and texture and to warm up the potentially chilly effect of the glass top.

Once you begin working with the four elements—wall decor, signature accessories, flowers and foliage, and ambience—you'll find yourself knitting the various elements together into a seamless whole. What you put on your wall relates to what you display on the table below. Candles, figurines, photographs and plants can be integrated into arrangements of collectibles and other accessories, contributing to the variety of shapes, heights, textures, and colors.

   In the pages that follow, you'll find practical information and inspiration to help you put these four elements to work in your own home. Ultimately, the goal is to establish an environment that fosters caring relationships and wonderful, loving memories. That's what decorating is all about. My own love of decorating stems from my love of home. I love being at home, and I know that my boys and my husband do, too. That to me is true success. Like my grandmother, I believe that creating a home that appeals to the senses on all levels is a way of showing your family how much you care about them. The four elements are guidelines to help you create a home environment that is all you hope and imagine it can be.

The coffee table is below eye level, so when you're seated, it naturally draws your eye (above). This makes it an ideal spot for showcasing special accessories. Displaying these items low, instead of in out-of-reach cabinets and bookcases, invites conversation and gives everyone the opportunity to enjoy them.

Sometimes less is more—with only a single figurine on one side of the mantel, attention focuses on the framed painting above it (opposite). The details that invite you closer—the photographs, books, flowers and art objects—are displayed on the tables. Candlelight and lamplight create the room's ambience. And when the temperature allows, nothing evokes the warmth of home like a fire in the fireplace.

WALL DECOR

In any room there are more walls than anything else. So the walls are a great place to start your decorating.

Fabulous furniture is wonderful, but a sofa will never rise to met your visitor's eye like a great wall display. Walls are hospitable. They are the first things your family and friends see on entering and the last things they spy when reaching for their coats. Whether you're at rest, work, or play, walls form the backdrop to your daily life. To establish the character of your home, use the walls as a wraparound canvas for personal expression.

The key to a truly harmonious home, however, is to look at the walls as an integral part of your decorating scheme rather than an empty space that needs to be filled. One or two paintings per wall, with an occasional mirror over the buffet or hall console, is the tired old formula. For a more distinctive look, avoid distributing your wall decorations evenly about the room and think instead of the role each display can play in the overall composition. The goal is a well-balanced mix of space, color, texture, and scale.

Start in FOCUS

In every room one wall inevitably attracts notice before all others. Some rooms have natural focal walls, which stand out with dominating features such as a fireplace, built-ins, or windows framing an attractive view outdoors. Most rooms, however, lack such prominent detailing, and the eye is drawn instead to a nondescript wall that stands behind a major furnishing, such as a sofa or master bed. Left empty such walls have a negative effect, making a room feel incomplete.

Well-accessorized focal walls set the stage for a successful design scheme. They are the decorator's equivalent to a personal invitation, drawing you into a space and urging you to take a seat. When creating your focal wall, think of your room as a stage and create a dramatic backdrop. Hang your largest, boldest decoration, or group together several pieces for impact. As you make your selections, consider style and mood. Your focal walls will serve as cornerstones for the look you build throughout your home.

A fireplace almost always takes the role of focal point; ordinary objects gain importance when placed on the mantel and the wall above (right). A grid of identically framed botanical prints emphasizes the seating area as the focal point of the room (opposite).

All in PROPORTION

Displaying artwork is an art in itself. Rather than forcing a favorite piece into focal point position, consider what type of display the wall space suggests. Proportions and scale are critical: A large painting can look cumbersome looming over a delicate spindle-back chair, for instance, and tiny objects may seem lost on a large expanse of wall. Choose artwork whose size and shape relate well to the wall and to nearby furnishings. A helpful ratio is 3:4. For example, the botanical print (*opposite*) is about three-fourths the width of the tray table below it. Stand as far back as possible to view your displays because the effects of scale are best seen in perspective. The eye also gauges the weight of decorative elements. As a general principle, choose wall hangings that appear lighter in weight than what stands below.

The painting poised above the tip of the antique birdcage (left) is about as wide as the base of the cage, so the two pieces have good visual balance. The print (opposite) is large yet light in color, so the delicate tray table stands up well beneath it.

The right
HEIGHT

If your eye has to travel too far upward,
the unity you want to exist between walls
and furniture will be thrown off.

Most people hang art too
high—maybe because it's more
comfortable to hammer in a
nail standing up, arm raised above the
shoulder. Or they may be tempted to center
a display in the available wall space.
Instead, think about how the room is
used. Is it a standing space, such as a
foyer (*below left*) or a hallway? If so,
position the wall display at standing eye
level. Is it a sitting room where you'll
view art from the sofa? If so, hang the art
low. This makes for comfortable viewing
and establishes a link between the wall art
and nearby furniture. To group several
pieces into one display, center the
composition at the proper eye level. The
highs and lows of nearby furniture and
architectural features are also helpful
guides. The wall display that combines a
mantel clock and paintings (*above left*)
loosely aligns with the door frame and the
top of the grandfather clock, reaching
down to the child's chair by the fireside.

Hanging artwork lower than expected
(opposite and above left) *invites viewers
to come close to enjoy it. In an entry,*
(below left), *hang something at
standing eye level.*

23

The right
FRAME

I f you want your art displayed to its fullest potential, consider its frame. A frame needs to pose enough contrast to make its contents stand out from a wall; at the same time it must harmonize with your art and the overall scheme of the room. This push-and-pull effect—between harmony and contrast—creates a visual tension that can enhance the impact of your art. Usually larger paintings are presented in heavier, more complex frames and smaller works in lighter, simpler frames. However, if your eye approves, break the rules and enjoy the results. Mats are typically used on drawings, prints, and watercolors. Choose mats that are wide enough to establish breathing space between the artwork and the frame. Neutral mat colors (white, off-white, and pale gray) almost always are effective choices; alternatively, a color from the print also works well. (However, if you notice the mat before the print, the mat is too strong in color.) Match texture to the nature of the subject: A suedelike texture looks handsome on hunting prints or black and white photos, while a petal-flecked mat or a mat with a ribbon texture is best for florals or botanicals.

The average width for a mat is about 3 inches all around. Going even wider gives the framed piece more breathing room.

A line DANCE

E very wall display takes direction. An emphasis on horizontal lines can create the illusion of width in a narrow room; horizontal displays usually are a sound choice for down-to-earth, casual decorating schemes. Vertical arrangements raise expectations of grandeur. The taller the arrangement, the greater its air of formality. Decide whether you want to work with or against the lines of your architecture, to emphasize balance or create contrast. Horizontal arrangements can look fresh and contemporary hung low under soaring ceilings. In a room with a standard 8-foot ceiling, a horizontal arrangement at chair rail level brings the eye low and creates a feeling of intimacy.

Diagonal compositions are a traditional choice on staircase walls where they help point the way upstairs. When viewed from an even plane, however, these offset compositions can be as fun as coloring outside the lines. Also consider arranging your wall accessories on a diagonal line near changes in architectural level or in an attic or a playroom with a sloping ceiling.

Let the architecture of a space guide the shapes of groupings: diagonal for stairways (above left), horizontal for wide expanses (below left), or vertical for slender spaces between windows (opposite).

Intriguing MATCHMAKING

Symmetrical arrangements soothe the eye. Such displays, when divided in half vertically, form two mirror images, creating a studied and refined look. If used over and over, however, symmetry can feel static; the eye longs for an occasional break from measured perfection. The wall display in the dining room *(left)* features platters with slightly different shapes and patterns in an otherwise symmetrical grouping. A clear focal point (the painting) anchors the group and gives it order. To create similar relaxed symmetry, begin with your strongest object at center, then spread out using pairs of items or items of equal visual weight. Above the mantel *(opposite)* the objects on each side of the central mirror are identical, establishing formal, balanced symmetry. Items on the mantel itself are almost identical—but not quite. The "not quite" loosens the otherwise formal balance. The candelabra on the left is balanced by a lidded, urn-shape container and wreath on the right. Creating equilibrium around a focal point without relying on mirror images offers the ease of symmetry minus the formality.

Symmetrical balance—mirror images on each side of an imaginary centerline—relaxes when you vary the shapes on one side of the line (left and opposite).

29

Working with PATTERN

*If your wallpaper has a busy pattern,
choose artwork and frames that
are calmer and quieter.*

Decorating plain walls is
relatively easy. Anything you
hang on them, whether framed
artwork, collectible china, or quilts,
supplies instant interest through pattern
and color. Patterned backgrounds pose
more of a challenge. You need to choose
items that contrast sufficiently with the
pattern to show up well. In fact, wall
decor against a patterned background is
most effective if it functions as an island
of nonpattern, a place for the eye to rest.

On the black and white wallpaper
(*opposite*) antique white platters, hung
back side out, offer relief from the busy
pattern. On the adjacent wall, a wide
white frame provides a generous margin
around a black and white photo so the
picture stands out amid the design. Even
against a subtly patterned backdrop like
the shutters (*right*), opt for simplicity in
your artwork. Wide mats provide
breathing space that lets your eye separate
the art from the background.

*If you love patterned backgrounds,
choose wall decor that is pattern-free or
surrounded by a wide frame or mat
(right and opposite) so the art stands out.*

Balance of POWER

Even the most carefully choreographed wall grouping can appear off balance if forced to compete for attention, so make potential competitors—architecture and furnishings—allies in your wall display. Imagine the entire wall as your canvas. Everything on or against it—including windows, doorways, plants, lamps, or furniture, for example—is an integral part of your composition. The number and variety of elements involved can make every addition to your wall a new balancing act. If you place a framed piece over one half of the sofa, for instance, balance it with a tall plant on the opposite side. If several elements overlap, treat them as a visual unit. In the wall arrangement (*opposite*) the shadow box frame in the lower right corner of the grouping is significantly smaller and lighter in weight that its companions. However, an umbrella stand and its collection of hats and canes help fill in the wall space around the small frame, giving that corner more visual weight to balance the composition.

A tall, airy tree softens the corner and balances the painting, which hangs closer to the window than to the corner (left). The umbrella stand (opposite) helps fill out the wall display and gives the space a sense of completeness.

Tricks with MIRRORS

Mirrors give rooms extra twinkle, creating double vision of the loveliest sort.

With mirrors, the art you frame is your room—only better. Carefully planned reflections can maximize available light, expand the sense of space, and bring heightened dimension to flat walls. Experiment: Use a large mirror to double your pleasure in a floral bouquet or an artful vignette, or cluster several small mirrors of different sizes and shapes for variety. Place mirrors carefully to avoid awkward reflections such as bare walls, the television, or a cluttered desk. To prevent startling passersby with their own image, avoid hanging mirrors straight-on from traffic corridors. Alternatively, tilt the mirror up or down for a change in perspective. Mirrors can enhance or disguise architectural features, helping to reshape space. In some cases they present strong focal points; they can also reverse lines of sight. In the living room (*below left*) a mirror placed between two prominent windows draws the eye away from the view outdoors and back toward the comforts of home.

Small mirrors reflect light in a corner (opposite). A convex mirror (above left) gains impact as the only round object on the wall.

Fascinating RHYTHM

My grandmother felt that women have to develop their own pattern for success—and this applies to home decorating too.

An accessory you love may be worth repeating, especially when you arrange similar objects in rhythmic patterns of shape, form, color or texture. Your eye takes in a room at a pace dictated by the objects on display; this pace is called visual rhythm. Rhythmic displays require repetition, which sets the eye in motion, and contrast, which is like the starts and stops of a catchy beat. For example, the weathered birdhouses and iron sconces *(above right)* echo each other in form (two rows) and color while offering subtle textural contrast. For a jazzier look, experiment with alternating patterns (using two or more repeating elements in an orderly sequence) or progressive sequences (in which an element rises or diminishes in strength or scale). Pay attention to spacing as well. Looser, gradual transitions will relax the visual rhythm of a display *(above left)*, while tighter spacing brings excitement to the mix *(below left)*.

Rectangular mirrors of different heights (opposite) step the eye from a high point down to the mantel. Repeating identical shapes (right and above) sets up a syncopated rhythm whose speed depends on the spacing between items.

The picture GALLERY

Small artwork makes a big statement when gathered into dynamic configurations modeled on Europe's oldest picture galleries. Kings and courtiers once crowded art on walls to convey the enormity of their collections or the depth of their connoisseurship. To adapt this approach to grouping, trust your eye: Some pieces seem to "go together naturally," while others stand apart. Establish unity by using the same color or style of frame; group the art by media (such as all photography or all drawings), subject matter, or dominant colors. To keep things interesting, choose pieces of different visual weights and sizes or use frames with different widths or textures. To ensure a sense of order, imagine drawing a line around the outside edges of the grouping. If it has a definable shape, the medley will feel unified. Following the outlines of nearby architecture or furnishings is another option; for example, in the bedroom (*left*), a picture gallery rises to follow the curve of the headboard. Spacing is a matter of personal taste. However, as a rule, avoid placing any object more than half its width away from a neighboring piece.

The photo grouping (opposite) looks unified because the frames—some old, some new, some carved, some plain—are painted white. The variety of frames styles adds visual interest and character.

Special
COLLECTIONS

My grandmother often said, "Love has a locale on earth—and it is called...home."

One accessory adds a touch of style; a collection displays true passion. Gathered together, your prize pieces can make a powerful, personal design statement—especially when displayed on walls where artwork takes on gallery status. Too much of any collection, however, can overwhelm a room, so edit for space and clarity, leaving each piece enough room to be fully appreciated. The best collections—like the best rooms—are built on principles of variety and unity. Select pieces that contribute to the group as a whole, yet speak up as individuals. Make displays accessible if they require close-up viewing. Or establish some viewing distance to heighten the overall impression a large-scale collection makes. Painted tole trays hung in a small bath *(left)* are doubly impressive thanks to a mirror that provides reflection and extended perspective.

Tole trays are ideal for wall decor (left), and with a little imagination, three-dimensional collections such as musical instruments can become wall art too (opposite).

In living COLOR

Color is the best mood setter in the decorating business. Bold or soft, fiery or cool, every hue affects your mood differently. In a mostly white room *(above right)*, art leads the way in determining the room's color personality; pillows, throw, and chairs pick up on the red, yellow, and blue hues. For a stronger color statement, paint the walls to match or contrast with your key upholstered pieces and select wall decor in a harmonizing color. Pistachio walls *(opposite)* are close to the color of the upholstered chair, creating a quiet but cheerful mood. Blue and white china and blue mats on the framed prints offer cool, crisp contrast to the yellow green; the draperies bring together shades of both colors to unify the room. The more color matches you make, however, the less freedom you have to introduce new treasures. For greater flexibility experiment with colors that are tints and tones of each other. The yellow and blue plates *(below right)* create the color story in this bedroom, and softer versions of the colors appear on quilts and cushion.

Wall decor emphasizes the room's color scheme by repeating colors in the accessories and upholstery (above right) *or by contrasting with wall and upholstery colors* (opposite).

Pure CONCEPT

There's adventure and satisfaction in assembling items that make a statement and bring delight to the people who live or visit within those four walls.

Every accessory you hang ought to stand out from your walls while blending with your overall decor. To achieve this look of "bold and blended," you need a consistent design scheme. Color schemes are a familiar example; other design schemes emphasize compatible materials, textures, styles, or shapes. For a personal look, consider using a theme approach. Let your personality, interests, or ideals guide your choice of wall accessories so they are in character with other belongings. Some themes are clear and direct (such as hanging starfish on the walls of your seaside retreat or matching your children's art to their bedsheets). The most intimate spaces, however, have subtler themes that are harder to define in a quick phrase. For example, a restful bath weaves together various elements associated with purity in nature and natural therapies: clean white linens, pressed foliage in frames, and a shelf of bottled bath products with an old apothecary look.

Art in the bathroom? Why not! Give yourself something lovely to look at while you soak. Moisture will eventually damage paper, so use inexpensive prints or artwork that can withstand steam or splashes.

Grounding your
ARRANGEMENTS

The happiest wall decorations will never leave you hanging. To avoid the "lost in space" effect, create a path that the eye can follow from the height of a wall hanging to a resting point near the floor below. For example "ground" or anchor a vertical row of paintings with a side chair *(above left)* or arrange a line of platters or plates above a narrow cupboard *(opposite)*. The eye starts at the floor and follows the furniture up to the wall display and then travels back down again. The key is to give the eye a path that connects the wall display to its environment. In your own home, a tall plant, floor lamp, or folding screen might serve the purpose. Alternatively, table lamps and bouquets can extend the reach of short furnishings, spanning the distance to artwork, mirrors, or other accessories hanging above *(below left)*. Placing anchor pieces off-center beneath your wall hangings provides a refreshing break from the formality of a straight vertical line. Note, too, how a lampshade can carve out wall space for a small framed piece that hangs low, just above the chair rail *(left)*. This unexpected placement puts the art at seated eye level and creates a feeling of intimacy.

Anchor vertical wall displays with a piece of furniture to integrate them into the overall decor.

Turning
POINTS

Why decorate one wall at a time when the goal is to wrap entire rooms in charm? Wall displays that turn corners anticipate roaming eyes. They can cozy sharp angles, dress an awkward niche, and create a gentler sense of flow through your home. The next time you find yourself standing in the center of a room pondering where to hang your newest accessory, do something different: Move around. Walk through your room as guests do at holiday parties. Watch how every corner, every angle throws artwork hung at the same height askew. Does your architecture defy your eye's craving for perfect symmetry? Three gilt frames on contiguous walls smooth an unexpected turn in this living room *(opposite)*, giving a sidelined mantel greater status by their presence. Do windows and doors pierce your walls, leaving small but noticeably empty corners? A chair and mirror-image sconces may provide a stylish solution *(left)*.

Lead the eye smoothly around a corner with focal-point art work on each wall (opposite).
Vases supported by hanging brackets bring a dark corner to life (left).

49

Accent
SHELVING

If you want a wall to reach out and make people take notice, add a shelf—or several.

Walls may be flat, but wall displays need not follow suit. Hanging three-dimensional objects creates visual interest; wall-hung brackets or shelves offer even greater depth. Whatever type of shelf you choose, it will have decorative value in its own right, in addition to its practical purposes. Ledges a few inches deep will project your treasures into the room, enlivening the displayed items with the play of light and shadow. Objects poised on a single bracket in the center of a symmetrical wall display can offer a resting place for eyes *(right)*. For extra volume experiment with a mix of flat and sculptural pieces, or build up groupings in layers *(opposite)*. Use the shelf space to lean some objects against others that are either standing or hanging behind. Sconces offer another option for adding depth to walls; the light they provide can have space-sculpting effects.

Brackets and wall-mounted shelves give wall decor dimension. If the shelf is deep enough, overlap and layer items to lead the eye in and out of the display (opposite).

A question of
SPACE

Eyes require a certain amount of wall space to fully appreciate each display and the individual items that make up a particular grouping. Spacing affects clarity and mood. Contemporary rooms require some open expanses while traditional rooms containing diverse patterns, colors, or tabletop accessories invite clustering and denser displays. In some cases a bit of breathing space can make a wall appear wider or a ceiling higher. The petite prints hung on the kitchen wall (*opposite*) stand back quietly in a busy corner work space; their size and positioning stretches the sense of perspective to make the room appear deeper.

Spacing is important in denser groupings too. In the bedroom (*left*), a mosaic of framed pieces is carefully composed to allow more space around the large, central print. This gives the grouping a clear focal point. The smaller pieces on each side hang closer together so the eye takes them in as a single unit. Their placement leads from the ceiling down around the bed, creating a strong center of interest.

Irregular spacing creates an active line for the eye to follow (left). For a calmer effect, allow more space around a pairing (opposite); keep the two pieces close enough that they look like a duo rather than two solo acts—about the width of one piece.

Secret WALLS

If you're short on wall space, check your rooms for walls in disguise.

If you wish you had more display space, remember that walls take forms other than painted plaster. Windows are really glass walls and can hold an attractive painting with ease. Tall folding screens are portable walls, and doors are walls that swing from one room to another. Floor screens and doors can host a variety of wall art—on both sides. Every vertical surface in every nook and cranny is a potential site for a wall display. The sites you choose can be as creative as the items you put on display. Tall bookcases or built-in shelves, for example, offer multiple surfaces to exploit. Layer your items over a few shelves (as if on an imaginary wall covering the cabinet front) or populate the recessed walls between the shelves with a series of miniature portraits *(left)*.

Hanging framed artwork over a window (opposite) works best if the backing is opaque. Light will show through paintings on canvas.

For interior designers a bare wall over a sofa is a blank canvas full of decorating possibilities. That same blank space for home decorators can be downright daunting: How high should I hang the pictures? What if I make a mistake and have exposed nail holes? How do I know where to hang what? In the following step-by-step instructions, you'll learn the secrets that interiors designers know; then you too can confidently build a wall display, choosing items that suit your personal style and budget.

Step 1

A well-balanced wall display is easy to build when you follow the "elements of three" design principle. First, position the largest component (here a square print) about 6 inches above the center of the sofa. This is the anchor of your display. Next, center a smaller framed piece above it, leaving a space about as wide as the larger frame (3 inches) between the two. Finally, top the pair with a visually lightweight, contrasting element (the iron scroll). Before you hang your art, create a map: Trace a rough outline of each piece onto brown kraft paper, cut out the shapes, and tape them to the wall. After you map out a pleasing arrangement, pull the picture wire on each piece taut, mark the nail position, and then drive the nails right through the paper for accurate positioning.

Step 2

As your budget allows, enhance your initial wall display with elements that add different shapes and textures. Like the iron scroll, the flowers and candle sconces offer curving contrast to the straight lines of the framed prints. Position the vase brackets near the top third of the lowest print and hang the candle sconces so the bottom scrolls are even with the bottoms of the vases. These elements widen the composition and carry the eye upward, unifying the arrangement. Leave about 5 inches between each of the new components to avoid crowding.

Step 3

For even more richness in texture and shape, add a pair of rectangular platters below the sconces and balance them with a pair of plates above. The platters create a strong horizontal base line that ties everything together. The plates punctuate the vertical elements and complete an imaginary arc that runs from candle to candle across the top of the grouping.

E ffective asymmetrical displays strike a balance by teaming unlike objects that have similar visual weight. Such a wall display might feature mismatched elements hung at differing heights in several colors; however, the various elements achieve dynamic equilibrium. Although such displays may look as if they came together by chance, in fact they are carefully planned.

Step 1

To build an asymmetrically balanced wall grouping above a chest or table, start with a basic mirror (or artwork) centered over the chest. The painted frame of this mirror brings color to the wall and echoes the clean lines of the chest below. Hang the mirror about 6 inches above the chest, or a little more than the width of the mirror frame; this spacing allows the eye to make an easy connection between the top of the chest and the wall display.

Step 2

Hang a wicker wall basket on the right side of the mirror. The long cylindrical shape contrasts with the rectangular mirror and fills the wall space above the chest. (In general, keep the width of the wall display within the bounds of the chest or tabletop to maintain good visual balance.) Position the basket so it's roughly centered between the top and bottom edges of the mirror and about 5 inches away from the edge of the frame. The shape of the flower arrangement is important too: The fluffy profusion of blooms in the basket adds softness that complements the cottage-style furnishings. A more vertical type of grass or flower would suit a formal or traditional setting.

Step 3

To balance the wall basket, choose two or three objects whose total visual weight equals that of the basket. Here, two painted plates introduce a new contrasting shape to the grouping; their floral design and creamy white background reflect elements already present in the display. Like the symmetrical wall displays on pages 56–57, this asymmetrical arrangement builds on the "elements of three" design principle, using one larger object on the right to balance two smaller objects on the left. In this grouping, the largest object is centered above the furniture as it would be in a symmetrical grouping; the supporting items are then arranged to create a balanced asymmetrical composition. For a more complex approach to asymmetry, shift the largest object to one side of an imaginary centerline and balance it with the three smaller items.

3

SIGNATURE ACCESSORIES

Accessories should be as individual as your signature, putting your personal stamp on a room and reflecting the things you love most.

Furniture and wall decor can set an attractive stage, yet ultimately you—your own design sensibilities—must get into the act to build a true home, a space that feels warm and personal. Signature accessories are objects that boldly declare or quietly reveal the essence of who are you. Much more than decorations, they are the design ingredients that make a room distinctly your own. Was it Audrey Hepburn's little black dress moviegoers adored, or was it the way she paired Givenchy with gloves, pearls, and her own offbeat charm? The mix is often more enchanting than the separate elements. Every object on display—from the contents of your bookshelves to keepsakes on a nightstand—contributes to the success of your decorating scheme. However, if you merely toss your accessories around the room, even your dearest treasures will appear as random filler. Place your accessories with thought, paying attention to color, patterns, forms, and textures; then step back and admire how your home sparkles with creative expression and personality.

The art of the VIGNETTE

Whether you're after bold drama or subtle softness, a touch of formality or casual ease, every vignette begins with basic architecture. Your largest or major vertical objects are the scaffolding; position these first. Next bring in medium-size and smaller objects to lead the eye from the verticals down to the tabletop and across its surface. Using a variety of shapes and sizes adds intrigue, but for visual ease limit the color scheme to one or two hues. Play with heights and depth, overlapping pieces to lead the eye into the display as well as across it. To knit a tabletop vignette to a wall display *(right, opposite, and pages 64–65),* layer objects from front to back and use the verticals to tie different levels together. For example, on the desktop *(right),* the lamp stands on a box, creating a resting point that weaves two tiers of the display along a serpentine path toward the central focal point, a painting hung on the wall behind. In the tabletop vignette *(opposite),* layered photos build up to the candlestick lamps, which carry the eye into the circular arrangement of plates and platters.

Move the eye from the front of the display toward the back by layering objects of different heights. Use color to unify objects of various shapes and sizes (see pages 64–65).

Color
LINKS

Color can burst on the scene in one bold stroke with dramatic results. Extra doses of the same color, repeated at intervals, can make your room pulse with lively rhythm. Signature accessories sometimes inspire the color scheme for an entire room. For example, a dining area painted and furnished with varying shades of soft green and white *(opposite)* takes its cue from a favorite set of green dinnerware. In other cases, accessories repeat and reinforce an existing color scheme. Purple gazing balls, for example, bring the color to the dining table *(below right)*, while the table runner, artwork, and other accessories add complementary yellow accents. In the living room *(above right)*, touches of blue in the lamp, rug, and painting repeat the strong wall color. Here the accessories act as mediators between the bold blue walls and the pure white upholstery and help to unify the various furnishings in the room.

Use accessories to add little dollops of the key colors in your palette. This repetition creates visual comfort.

Staying in SHAPE

Color is only one tool for establishing flow in a design scheme. Repeating similar shapes, forms, and patterns through accessories also creates a sense of connection often so subtle that it is sensed rather than consciously noticed. Shape is the two-dimensional outline of an object, whereas form is the object itself, a three-dimensional body. A floral hatbox, a straw boater, a vintage clock, an old sewing kit with spools, and a lamp with a fluted shade occupy the bedside table *(left)*; the various forms share the same shape—they are all basically round. Different shapes have different psychological effects. Circles suggest unity and continuity, while squares are considered sturdy and rational. Triangles communicate stability when the tops point upward, yet appear dynamic when set askew. When playing with shape, remember the rules of progression and emphasis. In the living room *(opposite)* scroll brackets function as wall art, echoing the shape of the vase on the side table, the playful arabesques in the upholstery, and the smaller leaf-inspired patterns on the blue and white Oriental pottery. This repetition creates subtle harmony in the room.

When deployed strategically, accessories with similar shapes carry out a crucial design mission: the creation of rhythm and unity in a room.

Contrasting TEXTURES

The friendliest interiors are approachable on every level. They feel warm and livable and strive to build your sense of physical and emotional comfort. Why is that nubby chenille blanket so appealing? For the same reason that a puppy pulls on your heartstrings—it begs you to reach out and touch it. Textural accessories make the comforts of your rooms more palpable. They breathe life and interest into a space, enriching surfaces with the play of light and shadows. From the dulled gleam of tarnished metals to the patina of gently worn woods, such subtle effects may not catch your attention as immediately as color or pattern. Yet when textures are layered for contrast, the rhythm they create is sustaining. Juxtapose rough against slick, hard against soft, and fibrous against silky to direct visual flow. These contrasts are particularly important in neutral color schemes, such as palettes of whites, grays, browns, or leafy greens. Monochromatic rooms can feel blissfully serene; contrasting textures keep them from dozing off into dullness.

All-white rooms (opposite and left) require variations in texture, from weathered wood to shiny porcelain, to feel warm and inviting.

Blend your SEAMS

Accessories are the key to linking the horizontal plane of your tabletops with the vertical expanse of walls behind. Look at the shapes, colors, patterns, and textures of your objects and play with arrangements to create a seamless visual path. Tabletop displays are like set dressings for the walls. Experiment with layers and heights to bring fuller dimension to the space, employing your objects like actors on a stage to create depth and drama. The triangle or pyramid is a helpful compositional tool: Build your display with this shape in mind, keeping the base relatively wide and using taller objects to mark the highest point *(opposite)*. Turn a few objects on their side if necessary or place an object on a stack of books to raise it to the desired level. Play horizontals against verticals to create balance. The proportions of your space and the mood you want to create can help you decide whether horizontals or verticals ought to dominate. A dining table *(right)* presents an inviting surface for a horizontal grouping of porcelain and silver; candles and branches provide balancing verticals that lift the eye toward the chandelier.

Put a tureen lid on a stand and it becomes an accessory (right). *The lamp defines the top of a triangle* (opposite), *and books and art are positioned to suggest a stable base.*

Create a
DESTINATION

Have you ever walked through a house where every piece of furniture was pushed against a wall? Even in narrow rooms, such arrangements lack intimacy. Pull your furnishings away from the wall to discover how much more inviting the room feels! Accessories play an important role in creating these welcoming layouts. Arranged in attractive vignettes on sofa tables, chests, and coffee tables, accessories become destinations defining distinct areas within a room and drawing people in. To create a destination within a room, imagine a fifth wall behind your display. Build your composition up into the airspace of the room if you want to make a statement. To assemble a vignette, use objects of at least three different heights (short, medium, and tall) to lead the eye from the table surface up into the air. Cluster small items on a tray or book to anchor and unify them. Arranging the porcelain sheep *(left* and *opposite)* on a low stack of books creates the effect of a presentation and emphasizes the importance of the figurines.

Tabletop displays create multiple destinations within a large living area (left). A roughly triangular shape leads the eye from the highest point to the table surface.

Living
LARGE

If your room has grand architecture and hefty furnishings, seek large-scale accessories that will complement the space. (If your furnishings are slim-lined and dainty, delicate small-scale accessories are more appropriate.) The room *(opposite)* features few accessories, but those few—the vase on the coffee table, the lamp, an orb on a pedestal, a print against the windows—are large-scale and simple in shape, echoing the style and visual weight of the larger furnishings. A large shallow tray collects books and magazines to keep the coffee table uncluttered. Trays can also display small items such as figurines. Gathered into a tray, they function as a single unit and therefore have more impact than a scattered collection.

The floor is an often overlooked display surface. Large urns or pieces of sculpture can fill a corner and anchor a floor-level display. A vintage glove form and artist's hand model *(left)* point the way from the floor to the top of the urn—and add a bit of fun to the clean-lined look.

In boldly scaled rooms, large-scale accessories provide the necessary visual weight to fill the space. Bold accessories work in small rooms too, serving as dramatic focal points.

Statuesque
BEAUTY

Definitely figure on figurines. Decorative
models of people, animals, birds, and
flowers add a delightful touch of life and
style to any tabletop or shelf.

Many people remember
Michelangelo for his paintings
in the Sistine Chapel.
However, the artist considered sculpture
his greatest creative endeavor. The way he
saw it, his figures were living in stone,
and his chisel merely freed them. Good
sculpture does bring its subjects to life; it
can also enliven a room. Statuettes,
ceramic models, plaster busts, tiny glass
figurines—all of these sculpted forms
bring a certain joy to a room. Place
figures at arm's length if you want them to
command attention (up on a mantel or
bookshelf, for instance) or gather them
within reach for greater intimacy. Placing
a few figurines on a side table, for
example, can relax the formality of a
traditional room. Use stacked books for a
pedestal and an ordinary table lamp for
your spotlight. Prop a small artwork
behind a figurine to give it a background.
Leave a little breathing room around each
piece to maximize its sculptural appeal.

*Medium-size and large figurines can stand
alone on desks, coffee tables, and dressers
(right). Or group pieces such as shepherdesses
and sheep as if to tell a story (opposite).*

Customizing your CABINETRY

Bookcases and shelves combine the functions of storage and display. A wall of built-in bookcases (*opposite*) sets off belongings like a series of shadow-box frames. Take advantage of this effect with a few added accessories: Place collectibles alongside your books or mix a few family photos with your best china. Edit carefully to build character rather than clutter. To achieve order and balance, treat every tier of shelving as an independent vignette while taking care to relate each one to the shelves above and below. Distribute your most substantial objects first, judging by visual weight rather than dimensions. (For example, small metal objects often look heavier than larger glass objects.) Use these weightier objects to anchor the display on each shelf. Add depth by layering: Lean some objects and stack others. Open an illustrated book and display it on a tabletop easel; or turn a teacup into a stunning silhouette against the backdrop of a propped-up saucer. As you work, step back occasionally and reshuffle items as necessary to balance the look. Casual, asymmetrical displays often require more careful choreography of colors, shapes, materials, and textures than formal, symmetrical ones.

Porch columns and a cornice cut from pine give a plain bookshelf architectural character (left). The center section of a wall of bookcases serves as a focal point (opposite).

Negative SPACE

Whether you use your bookshelves for books or for art and collectibles, consider the space around the objects—the negative space—as one of the key elements in your display. Even when you're working with little more than a collection of paperbacks, the bookshelf can become an eye-catching focal point if you paint the back panel a vibrant color *(right)*. On the shelves that are above the furniture line (the tallest chair back), arrange the books so the color shows through, laying some down to hold others upright. In effect you're carving the background color—the negative space—into shapes that draw the eye. If you prefer to use bookshelves as shadow boxes for your collections, remove some shelving to open up more space at the center of the unit. This will be the focal area, where your largest pieces will reside. On each shelf cluster objects for balance, pulling some forward and pushing others back for depth. Use repetition and variety to set up a pleasing rhythm across and up and down each set of shelves.

On book-filled shelves, (right), a bold background provides visual interest. A quiet backdrop lets the displayed items get all the attention (opposite and pages 84–85).

Hardworking
SHELVES

Odds and ends accumulate quickly in any household, making handy storage space essential. Yet even the most hardworking shelves can spare some room for style. Try out different containers to find the most attractive catchalls for your household necessities. Are you always running out of stamps in the office or paper napkins in the kitchen? Store them in view and you'll know at a glance when it's time to buy more. Pretty ceramic bowls, wallpapered hatboxes, silver vessels, richly textured basketry, and old wire bins are all stylish storage possibilities. Mix open and closed storage on exposed shelving for visual intrigue, reserving open bowls, bins, and baskets for daily-use items and using lidded containers for your archives and keepsakes. The goal of inventive storage is a look that's tidy but not rigid. Keep some spontaneity in your display, avoiding excessive symmetry. Visitors will take pleasure in your creativity; you and your guests may also feel some psychological comfort when you see how relaxed good organization can be.

Hardworking shelves look intriguing rather than chaotic because all of the objects, even the books, are arranged in blocks of neutral tones (opposite).

Utilitarian
UTOPIAS

The most heavily used spaces in a home—kitchens and baths—are often the least personal. These rooms are known for their function rather than their furnishings. Surfaces tend to be cold and hard: porcelain, granite, tile, metals, and mirrors. To make these spaces feel more friendly and comfortable, bring in accessories that add whispers of warmth and a punch of personality. Mix pretty, functional items—such as collectible pottery, vintage baskets, cookbooks, handmade soaps, and painted tins—with purely decorative objects. Add soft touches too, from delicate artwork to touchable linens. Look high and low for display space: The tops of your cabinets or a bare patch of floor could be a prime location for your treasures. Consider removing a few cabinet doors to expose shelving. (Kitchens and baths are already busy, so tidy displays are a must.) Use accessories that break up the monotony of hard surfaces. If your kitchen or bath is spacious, use accessories to create focal points that offer "destinations" for the eye and underline the idea of comfort in these utilitarian spaces.

Coordinating bowls and platters look like fine collectibles when artfully displayed on open shelves. Attractive containers keep everyday tools handy yet hidden from view.

Pretty and PRACTICAL

Two types of accessories make up most displays: functional belongings (books, coasters, and lamps, for example) and purely ornamental items (such as pictures, sculpture, or art objects). The most appealing vignettes often integrate both, hinting at the pleasure of daily routines. Are you on the hunt for a new address book, bedside journal, or telephone? If so, keep in mind the colors and furnishings in the rooms where the new item will be used. Everyday objects deserve to be selected as carefully as any decorative piece. Add a little art to their display. For example, pose a small ornamental figurine next to some perfume bottles or place a seashell beside plush bath towels. Kitchens and baths are particularly good places to make a display of everyday necessities. Begin by removing barely used items from all tables and countertops. Sort your must-haves by function and stow them in attractive open bins, bowls, or baskets. Clear containers can hold items with patterns and textures interesting enough to serve as art.

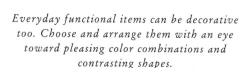

Everyday functional items can be decorative too. Choose and arrange them with an eye toward pleasing color combinations and contrasting shapes.

Table
MANNERS

Attractive table settings can make meals more pleasant and dishes more delectable. Accessories add fun and flair to a dining area and often become memory makers for your family and friends.

A home-cooked meal offers comfort. Add a well-dressed table to your efforts, and the result is a gesture of love. With only a few extra touches, you'll set your guests at ease and make the simplest occasions memorable. Choose accessories that have personal meaning and/or appealing color, shape, or texture. Anything goes—whether intended for dining or not. If the occasion is formal, lighten the mood with mismatched plates, an odd number of candles, and loose gatherings of your favorite collectibles. Keep your compositions flexible for a relaxed mood, and vary heights for interest. Old leather-bound books and two floral arrangements on this dining table *(left)* make the formal, European-style setting appear cozy and romantic. Instead of striving to impress your guests, focus on creating a lively conversation piece that expresses your joy in the occasion.

Have fun with the centerpiece by combining unexpected items (left). Glassware covers (opposite) originally kept flies out of the drink; now they're purely a pretty flourish.

Everyday
TABLESCAPES

Why wait until supper to set the table? Indulge your whims between meals with an everyday vignette and watch your family's reaction. A room with a mostly empty table at center stage is a wasted opportunity to create a sense of welcome. A few artfully arranged accessories can turn your underused dining room into a pleasant stop for morning coffee, homework, or afternoon conversation. Mealtime decorations are usually minimal, leaving room for serving dishes and plates. For the off-duty tablescape, think larger and spread things out. Without food on the table, you have room for a stronger focal point. Asymmetrical arrangements are generally more informal and more inviting than strictly symmetrical ones. Creating tablescapes is fun because it often involves using everyday items in unexpected ways. Here a cake plate rests on a platter and serves as a pedestal for a collection of candles. The candles stand on a bed of small pears held in place by the glass cylinder. Fruit and moss cover the platter, giving it enough visual weight to balance the candles.

The basic centerpiece of candles and fruit can stay in place during meals. The flowers and figurines fill out the display when diners depart.

The COFFEE TABLE

Whether you call it the coffee table or the cocktail table, this ubiquitous piece of furniture offers more than a horizontal surface for refreshments. Standing front and center in most living rooms, it serves a place to rest your eyes—and sometimes tired feet— bringing attention to the central function of the space: relaxation. The way you accessorize your coffee table says a lot about how you live. What do you need from your living room? Is this where the family catches up at the end of the day, or is it primarily a place for guests? Scatter books, flowers, and candles casually (though not randomly) for a relaxed cottage-style look *(opposite)*, and no one will worry about disturbing your arrangement when setting down a glass or morning newspaper. Tight arrangements positioned off-center *(right)* offer a more contemporary look. Including some height in the composition creates an interesting lift in the middle of the room; in general, however, keep the display low so natural focal points get due attention and people can see each other across the table.

A tightly grouped coffee table display conveys orderliness (right), *while a sprawling arrangement expresses cottage comfort* (opposite).

The Right
HEIGHT

Coffee tables usually stand about 20 to 24 inches tall, placing the tabletop at about the level of the sofa seat cushions. This puts teacups or books within easy reach when you're seated, and it's generally a comfortable height if your coffee table doubles as an ottoman. Tables taller than the standard height can serve as coffee tables too. A pedestal table *(left)* offers a surface for books and collectibles as well as a spot for writing notes and having tea. The unexpected height can raise the interest level in the room, inserting a peak where you normally expect a valley. Take advantage of this prominent position to create a display of favorite things. Even a table just a few inches taller than seat level can introduce an inviting intimacy to your room. The Asian-inspired table *(opposite)* paired with low contemporary chairs could become an impromptu dining table. To determine the height that's right for you, think first in terms of comfort and then consider whether the table relates well to your seating pieces.

Bring in a pedestal table from the sidelines to serve as a coffee table that doubles as a desk or dining spot. Choose accessories that are attractive from all sides—vases, sculpture, or books rather than framed pieces.

Side TABLES

A room may have several natural focal points—a fireplace, a view outdoors, great art, and a conversation area, for instance—yet these star attractions always rely on a cast of supporting players. Though by definition they stay on the sidelines, side tables play an important role in almost every room of the house. They serve as quiet areas, rest stops for the eye as it travels around the room. Use side tables as opportunities to combine functional items (lamps, for example) with objects you enjoy looking at. The goal is to create an engaging vignette that blends with the prominent colors and textures in the room and helps establish high and low points that lead your eye through the space. Avoid overcrowding. Your display ought to attract some attention yet remain content in the shadow of a focal point.

A modest side table display lets the focal point take the starring role (left). A side table serves up task lighting (opposite); decorative accessories play a supporting role.

Be FLEXIBLE

Art objects and other accessories are the jewels of your home. Like earrings and necklaces, they take on new sparkle and zest when they're rotated and incorporated into ever changing ensembles.

Have you ever visited a home so perfectly appointed that every element, every object seems precisely planned? If you felt nervous or awestruck, consider yourself perceptive: You instinctively recognized that too much control crowds out comfort and relaxation. It's wise to establish a color palette and overall design scheme for your rooms; however, a little flexibility will relax the look, giving you the option of making changes. Exact matches are unnecessary. Accessories in near-matching or contrasting hues and patterns let you redecorate on a whim. Formal settings benefit from a subtle break in symmetry or from the gentle surprise of an item used out of context—a teapot holding flowers or a china saucer as a soap dish. The goal is to create depth and variety in displays so your home looks as if it evolved over time. This seeming spontaneity will make your rooms inviting and intriguing—never intimidating—for guests.

A dramatic contemporary poster jazzes up classic blue and white porcelain (left). The pillows on the chairs and sofa (opposite) harmonize without matching exactly, creating a casual, collected-over-time look.

Embrace the
SEASONS

Temperatures, colors, and the quality of light all change with the seasons. This suggests an exciting thought: Mother Nature redecorates all year long—and so can you! Welcome in the outdoors by changing your accessories with the seasons. You wouldn't wear white sandals and breezy linens in the depths of winter, so why rely on the same woolen pillow come spring? Warm or cool your room by adjusting colors, materials, and textures. In winter layers of tablecloths and a color scheme of navy, red, and golden yellow convey warmth *(right)*. For spring and summer uncover the table and slipcover the chairs with tailored white skirts for a fresh, breezy feeling *(opposite)*. Wall decor supports the shift from winter to summer too, with botanical prints and decorative plates replacing the heavy patina of old oil paintings. Bring out brasses and warm woods in the fall, velvety reds in winter, and ocean blues in the summer. Even minimal changes can have impact: The same glassware on a sideboard can hold dyed eggs in the spring, dried leaves in the fall, and pinecones in the winter.

A change of colors, carried out in fabrics, artwork, and accessories, takes the room from winter to summer.

A touch of BLACK

Here's a decorator's secret: Every room needs at least a bit of black to ground its overall scheme. Think how a black frame sets off the colorful forms in a painting. Black sharpens edges, silhouettes shapes and textures, and increases the eye's perception of depth by throwing lighter tones into higher relief. When arranging your shelves or tabletop vignettes, consider harnessing the power of black as a backdrop. Pair it with dark colors for a hint of depth or with whites and bright tones for crispness. A black and white photograph anchors the vignette while drawing out the dark and light variations in the rich wood grain of the table *(left)*. The impact of black will vary according to its shade and texture. Experiment with glossy ceramics, wrought-iron candlesticks, and the traditional tole lampshade. Remember that a little black goes a long way. Too much dark can make a display moody, while a dash in the right place brightens and sharpens a composition.

A touch of black adds depth and satisfying drama to almost any room. Black is especially effective in a house with white walls and dark woodwork (opposite). Black accents tone down the stark contrast between dark and light.

Go with the
GLOW

Crisp white is a popular paint trim color—and always has been. Fine white china with a slight rim of silver or gold is a traditional choice. What's the reason?. Reflective metals, mirrors, clear glass, and brilliant whites are easy mixers in any decor, yet at the same time, they actively stir things up. They set off colors, multiply the effects of available light, and add a special spark to your everyday displays through their reflective qualities. Perhaps that's why cut crystal on the table or a silver tea service on a sideboard always catches the eye. The effects of light are engaging and mood-inspiring. Add a mellow glow to a casual, neutral palette via warm brasses and tarnished pewter or inject a touch of formality with polished silver accents. For maximum effect place these objects near a mirror or window. Alternatively, mix them in among a display of warm, earthy woods and natural fibers for contrast. Along with a dash of dark, every room needs a few flashes of brilliance—white, glass, or metal—to highlight its style.

Enhanced by lamplight, silver, gold, and crystal accessories add sparkle to your room and attract the eye to tabletop displays. And yes, silver and gold do mix!

In good HUMOR

Whether your style is casual or formal, traditional or contemporary, a few fanciful objects can refresh your decorating scheme. Old toys, folk art, garden ornaments, and figurines in the shape of your family pet are examples of accessories that can lift spirits on a dull day. Mix one or two into a table display that features precious objects or frame a child's drawing to fit in with books and photos on a shelf. Let these items catch your friends and family by surprise and watch how the unexpected draws them in for a closer view. Children's art makes a happy and playful display on a mantel *(above right)* and mixes easily with framed prints and a windup toy *(below right)*. Looking for an even more subtle approach to inject your personality into a room? Study traditional English decorating and American country decor. Both styles use objects out of context, relying on ingenious placement to bring playfulness to a space. In a living room a large bronze of spaniels curls up under the tea table, where a real dog might choose to rest *(opposite)*.

Fanciful touches lighten the mood (above *and* below right). *Books frame displayed figurines with contrasting color* (opposite).

Masterful MIXES

O ne of the delights in decorating is finding happy pairings between the things you love. Accessories gathered over time make a space feel warm and welcoming to you and your guests. A house becomes a home when it expresses who you are and what you love; its rooms will look as if they have grown with you, and furnishings will reveal something about your interests and your evolving tastes. Displays that employ juxtapositions of styles, periods, price-points, and mood are both exciting and highly personal. Look for common denominators, such as repeating colors, shapes, patterns, and textures. The gilded architectural bracket on the coffee table (*opposite*), for example, echoes the curvy shape of the teapot sculpture beside the fireplace. One is classical in style and one contemporary; the eye links them because they have similar shapes. Contrasting shapes can make special pieces stand out. In the living room (*left*), tall candlestick lamps and a geometric print hung on the wall create a grid that frames a curvy contemporary sculpture, giving it more emphasis.

Use contrasting shapes, such as the candlestick lamps and organic sculpture (left), *to highlight special objects. Use repeating shapes, such as the salvaged architectural bracket and the teapot sculpture* (opposite), *to create unity in a room.*

Search HIGH and LOW

I f you have carefully weighed all your accessories for color, size, and scale and something still seems lacking, look high and low. Your room has many surfaces other than tables and shelves. The tops of hutches, a windowsill, a stair landing, a footstool, a stack of books by the bed, or a bare patch of floor—all present viable opportunities for exciting new levels of display. In addition to horizontal balance, every room needs points of interest at various heights to achieve a sense of vertical balance. Place a few objects above eye level—platters, plants, books, or even a mirror, for example—to dress up cabinet tops and raise the eye toward the ceiling. In homes with cathedral ceilings, vertical displays can make a soaring space feel more connected to your furnishings. In less spacious rooms, leading eyes up and down the visual path of your displays makes the area feel roomier.

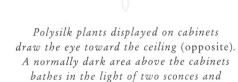

Polysilk plants displayed on cabinets draw the eye toward the ceiling (opposite). A normally dark area above the cabinets bathes in the light of two sconces and a mirror (left).

The great OUTDOORS

In the summertime living rooms take a step outside. Porches, decks, and patios are anchored by seating areas, so why not accessorize these as you would indoors? While comfortable furniture brings the indoors outside, your accessories can bring the outdoors in. Choose objects that connect your interior design with views of natural scenery. If the yard is woodsy, display a few objects in warm tones and textures, juxtaposed with greens and crisp summer whites. If you live on the coast, watery blues and golden sand colors conjure thoughts of a nearby beach. Forget about perfection: An exact color match or a clean surface will quickly change when exposed to the sun and the elements. Look for surfaces that will take on a friendly patina in the open air. In general keep the look loose and casual and your groupings flexible, bearing in mind that this multifunctional space will host everything from afternoon naps to outdoor suppers.

Take indoor comfort outside with comfortable seating and a place to put your feet up, but don't stop there. Accessorize porches and decks with lamps, collectibles, and rugs to create a welcoming space.

Share the
JOY

Ask youngsters, teens, or older family members who live with you to help pick out accessories. Draw everybody in and expand your thinking to encompass every nook and cranny, every kid and granny.

Another way to think about collections and accessories is to consider them your "memory makers." Decorate tabletops, mantels, and chests with objects that remind you of places you've been, people you love, and experiences you cherish. Let these memory makers be the backbone of your decorating and introduce variety with flowers, topiaries, and collectibles that you can change from time to time. In this room a model ship, a handmade quilt, spiral-turned candlesticks, and a colonial-style table lamp express a love of New England heritage and a strong sense of place. Topiaries in classical shapes and a flower bucket full of hydrangeas and lilies add a touch of life; they can easily be replaced with potted plants and pitchers of fresh or dried flowers for a change of pace.

Each surface in this room supports a simple display of just a few objects. The effect is cohesive but not cluttered, and it's easy to make changes if a new accessory comes home.

119

Decorating a room is much like working a puzzle. Once you have the frame in place, it's easier to tell how the other pieces fit. Starting with an attractive wall display gives you boundaries—a frame for carrying your decorating scheme from the wall to tabletops and other surfaces in the room.

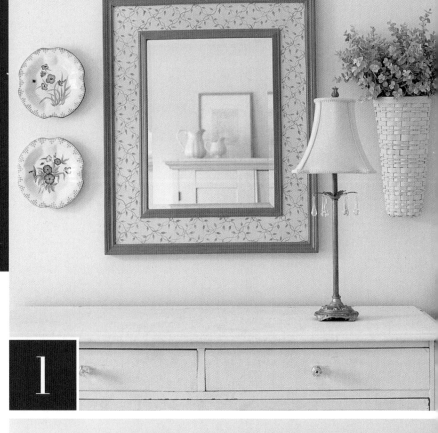

Step 1

The first building block in this tabletop display—a lamp—has practical and aesthetic value: It provides light (a necessity in a foyer) and ties the wall display to the table. Choose a lamp that corresponds with the scale and style of the furniture. This bronze lamp extends a little more than halfway up the side of the mirror frame, and its vintage style suits the cottage look of the wall display. In a more formal setting, choose a more substantial and detailed lamp.

Step 2

To balance the tall lamp, add something of similar (but not identical) height on the other side of the mirror. Here an urn filled with lacy ferns provides a different shape as well as a touch of color. A smaller urn leads the eye down to the tabletop. Compared to the lamp, these vessels are chunky; however, the visual heft of the wall basket helps balance the composition. A long, low tray for keys, mail, and sunglasses traces a horizontal line of color across the tabletop and leads the eye from side to side. The urn and the lamp frame the mirror, drawing attention to it and the reflected

space beyond. The openness of the composition emphasizes a spare, architectural quality.

Step 3/Options

An alternative tabletop grouping shifts attention from the mirror to a vase and a set of ferns, which are placed front and center on the chest. The mirror now serves as a frame for the greenery. Books standing upright balance the lamp. Chosen for their shape (strong verticals), color (neutral), and height, the books lead the eye up from the chest to the wall display; they also act as visual steps leading to the graceful foliage. In this grouping the eye follows a gentle arc that starts low on the left and rises to the tip of the lamp on the right. The effect is graceful rather than dramatic and romantic rather than architectural. Combining tabletop groupings and wall displays is an effective way to create secondary focal points in a room. Give yourself fresh views by changing the items on the tabletop and rearranging your display.

3

Bookshelves can hold much more than books. Indeed, rows of ordinary shelving offer an opportunity for you to showcase your collections, photographs, art, and accessories. The biggest temptation, however, is to cram too much on one shelf. Instead, think about the best placement for your favorite pieces; then arrange the display as a supporting cast.

When you choose accessories for decorating shelves, pick what brings you pleasure, what brings a twinkle to your eye, what makes your children smile, what makes your spouse say "Hey, I like that." Pick objects that reflect your interests, that show off hobbies, skills, or family history. Pick objects that mean something to you and those you love.

Step 1

Rather than attempting to rearrange the various items on your shelves, start fresh: Clear off the shelves completely. This is a good time to do a little decluttering if necessary. Sort through books, weeding out the volumes you no longer use, and donate them to a charity. Toss any outdated catalogs or magazines. Separate the remaining items into piles, stacking books and magazines of the same size and laying out artwork that you want to incorporate into the arrangement. You may need to recruit some accessories from elsewhere in the house to add interesting colors and shapes.

To begin creating your new display, remove the second shelf from the top (if you can) to accommodate large artwork. Arranged at standing

Before

eye level, these larger art pieces will be the focal point of the display. Choose a couple of large colorful pieces for one of the new spaces and layer them, leaning the first one against the back of the bookcase *(left)*. (If necessary use putty or soft wax to secure the frame to the shelf.) If a piece needs more height to fill the space well, prop it on a tabletop easel. Place artwork only on the upper shelves where people can see it without stooping.

Working from the top shelf down on each bookcase, stagger the placement of the framed pieces so they lead the eye on an interesting back-and-forth path. Also position pieces so they relate to those on the adjacent bookshelf. Angling framed pieces across the inside corners provides transition from bookshelf to bookshelf.

1

Step 2

The second layer of accessories introduces color, texture, and different shapes. Curvy vases in black and white patterns and solid chartreuse come from elsewhere in the house to complement the red and yellow colors in the prints. A pair of ceramic balls on a tray brings the black and white theme over to the left bookcase. A tall clock balances the tallest vase and pairs up with a silver alarm clock that once was hidden among the books. Linen- and paper-covered boxes, stacked for storage, introduce new textures and solid blocks of color on the lowest shelf. (Put fresh flowers in one of the vases from time to time, whenever you want to treat yourself. Or for a consistent color accent, rely on polysilk stems.)

Step 3

It's time to add the books. Group them by height and lean them against the sides of the bookcases. Also stack volumes to use as pedestals, adding depth and interest to the display. Notice how raising one vase in each of the vase pairs creates a more interesting line for the eye to follow (*opposite*). The small clock in the left-hand bookcase also gains stature, thanks to a stack of small books. To give the shelves a neater, more organized look, position all the books at the front edge of the bookcases instead of pushing them to the back; this emphasizes the books as blocks of color.

2

3

From one coffee table, four distinctly different looks emerge. Assembling a tablescape on the coffee table is a good way to reinforce the color scheme or mood of a room. Choose elements that express your sense of style. Flowers, vases, books, bowls, trays, collectibles, and candles are the tools you'll use to craft a pleasing focal point for your family room or living room.

Marvelous Monochromatics

Monochromatic means having only one color or hue. In this room caramel, amber, and shades of beige combine with soft white to create a serene space that beckons you to sit quietly and be. When you're limiting your palette to tints and shades of one color, texture and detail become critically important.

- Establish high and low points on each surface and remember to work from front to back and from side to side to create a variety of levels. Here amber vases filled with wispy yellow flowers mark the high point of the display.

- Stacks of books serve as pedestals for items from the kitchen and dining room. Chosen for their texture (shiny silver and glass versus dull eggs) and shapes, the items become art objects in this new setting. (Use brown ceramic eggs or opt for real ones: Poke a small hole in each end of the egg and blow out the contents. Wash out the interior; let them air-dry.)

- Pillar candles on a rectangular tray filled with pebbles add ambience as well as cylindrical shapes that echo the amber vases.

All About Color

Bright red, bold yellow, and chartreuse green form the foundation for this punchy tabletop display.

- The most eye-catching accessory, the round Murano glass vase filled with sunflowers, dictates the color scheme for the table. Two linear green vases displayed at different heights in the center of the table contrast with the shape of the larger vase.

- A crimson footed bowl filled with oranges and lemons repeats the warmth of the sunflowers, and a chartreuse tray lined with three red votives adds horizontal dimension.

- Colorful art books intensify the color scheme. They serve as a pedestal on the tabletop and stack neatly in red leather trays on the lower tier of the table.

Tantalizing Texture

Wrought iron, foliage, wicker, books with weathered covers, and textured candles come together for a pleasantly informal arrangement.

- Lanky bear grass, curvy branches, and sprigs of pussy willow spill out of a stately Grecian urn, creating a study in shape and contrast.

- Unusual trays serve in unexpected ways. The top tray, a footed wrought-iron stand generally used for plants, holds bright green spheres. The wicker and wood tray beneath, low-slung on stubby legs, is the perfect container for a stack of weathered books.

- With their rough-hewn, weathered appearance, the books contribute an important textural element.

Botanical Beauty

A soft green palette evokes a romantic mood in this botanical tablescape. Repetition and simplicity are key to the success of this look.

- Flowing ivy and the spare beauty of an orchid tucked inside a clear cylindrical vase command center stage. Placing the slender vase on a solid-color plate keeps the orchid from looking top heavy.

- A stack of garden-themed books elevates a clear glass compote that's filled with water and floating candles. A tall, pierced ceramic votive holder complements the curves of the compote and supplies a column of solid color that helps anchor the collection of glass on the tabletop.

- Rectangular baskets on the bottom shelf keep books and magazines tidy. The coarsely woven textures add warmth, grounding the tablescape of clear glass and ceramics above.

indoor gardening Diana Yakeley

Cynthia Gibson   A Botanical Touch

Gardens in France

Building a beautiful display in a kitchen or breakfast room lends elegance to these utilitarian spaces. And the beauty of such a display is that it turns your everyday dishes into an artful composition. Plain white dinnerware inspired the arrangement on this classic baker's rack. Use the principles of display—repetition, variety, balance, and layering—to create arrangements that please your eye.

Step 1

Start with the largest items, resting platters and a pair of plates against the back of the rack. To create depth, elevate a smaller, patterned platter on a plate stand so that it's framed by the large white platter. Position a pair of canisters front and center to balance the larger platter below. Note that the grouping forms an inverted triangular shape, which is dynamic but unstable. To help provide a feeling of stability, anchor the display with dark, visually heavy items: a wicker box and basket placed on the lowest shelf. Use only a pair of items to keep the look clean. The wicker box provides storage for linens and place mats, and an ivy plant in the wicker basket softens the hard lines of the baker's rack.

Step 2

To further stabilize the inverted triangle, frame the platters with upright books and a stack of plates. Scale comes into play with the addition of coffee mugs and stacks of bowls on the top shelf. Using the smallest items on the top shelf obeys the law of gravity; placing large items on this shelf would make the display look top heavy. The mugs and bowls also stretch the line of color horizontally.

Step 3

Add depth and color with containers of fruit and flowers placed in front of plates and platters. Fill bowls with fresh or artificial fruit, one type and color per bowl, and use pitchers to hold fresh or polysilk flowers. Avoid positioning similar objects along the same vertical line, one above the other. The goal is to lead the eye on a zigzag line down the shelves. On each individual shelf, place objects so they guide the eye up and down and in and out of the display. Fill in any holes. Here the wicker bottle beside the platters balances the books on the left and adds a touch of textural contrast.

3

Wall-mounted shelves and cabinets offer still more opportunities for arranging functional and decorative accessories. Because cabinets are primarily storage pieces, you may be tempted to pack them with assorted dishware. Resist the urge! Instead treat glass-fronted cabinets like prime real estate: Allow only a select few items to reside there, and keep plenty of open space around each unit to preserve the view.

Before

After

Cabinet Display

If your cabinet has glass doors or open shelves, select and arrange items to create a pleasing, orderly display. Here colorful items are tucked out of sight, and quieter white and silver tableware step in for a more refined look. (The display ideas presented here work equally well for colorful dishware and glassware.)

On the large center shelf, a platter, a teapot, cups, and a mug of flowers supply a focal point for the cabinet. A silver tea set, hidden in a corner cubby before, now takes center stage on the shelf beneath. Give your prettiest pieces some breathing room so they can be seen and appreciated.

A line of silver cups on the top shelf establishes rhythm; shifting the row off-center keeps it from looking too predictable and rigid.

Stacking teacups on saucers instead of on each other creates an interesting look, alternating curves and straight lines. Neat stacks of plates on each side of the tea set create a resting place for the eye.

Shelf Arranging

Creating an effective shelf arrangement is as easy as 1-2-3. The principles illustrated here apply to wall-mounted shelves, bookcase shelves, and mantels.

Step 1

Place one visually heavy item at each end of the shelf. Objects gain visual weight if they are large, colorful, dark, patterned, or unusually shaped. Here a large, curvy bracket anchors the shelf on the left, and the dark brown book provides equivalent visual heft at the other end.

Step 2

Add height and color. Tall objects emphasize vertical movement and add excitement. When you're decorating a shelf or mantel, align vertical objects with the shelf brackets so they visually connect with and extend the architecture. Color adds depth and interest. The light green vase echoes the color of the bowl, while the dark green vase balances the brown book.

Step 3

Use smaller items to bridge any gaps between the larger objects. The stack of wooden bowls are all similar in color, so they function as a single object. They repeat the brown of the book, creating unity in the display. The green balls add texture, and the finial plays off the teardrop shape of the dark green vase.

FLOWERS AND FOLIAGE

Every room of your house can benefit from the freshness of flowers, the prettiness of plants, and the glory of greenery.

Flowers and greenery bring immediate life to any room. Alfresco, the Italian word for outdoors, literally means "in the freshness." Bring freshness into your life by importing a bit of the outdoors into every room of your home. Whether you prefer fresh, polysilk, or dried greenery, choose (or create) arrangements that complement the overall decor of each room, including fabrics, wallcoverings, and furnishings. Greenery and floral arrangements can enhance the ambience of your rooms by drawing attention to favorite furniture and artwork. They can also be used to disguise awkward structural supports, soften dark corners, and balance furnishings.

GARDEN Rooms

Any space can feel like a garden room when you make greenery part of the decor. Movable planters such as wicker baskets on stands *(opposite)* give you flexibility: Take them out to the porch in warm weather and bring them in to a sunny room in winter. Flowering plants and grasses grown in terra-cotta pots blur the boundary between inside and out *(right)*. Wicker furniture and garden ornaments enhance the garden feeling.

If you travel frequently or have pets or allergies that prevent you from growing live plants, or if you merely want to avoid plant maintenance, consider using impostors—lifelike polysilk greenery and flowers. They are often more affordable than their living counterparts, and they're perfect for creating seasonal arrangements that can come out every year. To make polysilk stand in effectively for living plants, shape and bend the stems, leaves, and petals to mimic fresh foliage.

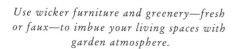

Use wicker furniture and greenery—fresh or faux—to imbue your living spaces with garden atmosphere.

The Art of
PLANTSCAPING

Decorating with plants takes as much planning as other types of composition. With living plants consider how much light and humidity each plant needs. Once you've identified the locations where your plants will thrive, start arranging the specimens into pleasing groupings of different heights, shapes, textures, and shades of green. In the grouping on the kitchen table *(left)*, a topiary provides height. Flowers step the eye down to the tabletop. When you're plantscaping a whole room, place plants at different heights to define an interesting path for the eye to follow. In the dining area *(opposite)*, plants rest on the floor, on a small table, and on a plant stand, providing fresh color and texture at several levels. (Apply the same arranging principles to polysilk plants without concern for light and humidity requirements.)

Match the scale of your plants to the location. In the kitchen (left) small and medium-size pots of flowers and ivy suit the size of the table. In the garden room (pages 140–141) the topiaries are tall and weighty so they balance the large-scale armillary spheres and architectural pieces that serve as sculpture.

Lush or SPARE

When you decorate with flowers, use light and shadow to enhance the effect the blooms have on your decorating scheme. Arrange flowers in places where sunlight streams in to cast dappled shadows, or where your lighting fixtures throw patterns of dark and light.

Design plantscapes to reflect your personal style. Do you love the comfortable, put-your-feet-up look of cottage style? The lush, flowers-everywhere approach (*opposite*) will appeal to you. Miniature trees and large plants work as design elements, filling corners and calling attention to architecture. If your style is formal, choose plants with strong linear quality, such as orchids and flowering branches (*above left*). For a look somewhere in between, combine dramatic foliage (fresh or polysilk), flowers, and live plants, and group them in one area, such as on a baker's rack (*below left*).

If a room has lots of natural light, place potted flowers on tiers of shelves in front of the windows (opposite). *The trompe l'oeil (French for "fool the eye") painting over the mantel* (above left) *adds hydrangeas to the mix of plants in the room.*

143

Color MATCHING

The most successful flower arrangements mix and match with the colors in your home. In a room with a multicolor scheme (yellow, blue, and white, for example) monochromatic arrangements provide a resting place for the eye (opposite). Single-color flower arrangements are also ideal for creating sophisticated displays of such formal flowers as roses and gardenias.

Using flowers in a range of related shades takes the monochromatic arrangement one step further. Hot pink, salmon pink, and red gerbera daisies (above right) give an overall impression of red, but the variations in color add interest and complexity. You can achieve a similar effect by choosing analogous colors, which lie next to each other on the color wheel.

One-color arrangements are dramatic. In general, however, a flower arrangement gains impact when you add at least a touch of opposing color. Warm colors (red, orange, yellow) need a dash of a cool hue (blue, purple, green), and vice versa; the contrast gives the combination snap.

Green bells-of-Ireland and flowers and berries in shades of red illustrate the impact of paired color complements (below right). Yellow flowers make the blue in the china look brighter (opposite).

Mood MAKERS

Some palettes lighten and brighten your mood; others calm it. Learning these color characteristics will help you choose flowers that enhance the ambience of your rooms for everyday living or for special occasions.

• Active colors include such warm tones as yellow, orange, and red. These color extroverts step out into a room to dominate the decor. They inspire conversation and an upbeat attitude.

• Passive colors such as cool blues, greens, and lavenders have a calming effect. They're ideal for bedrooms, private retreats, and tranquil getaways (a three-season porch, for example). In a room with a neutral backdrop, cool-color blooms draw the eye to a focal point in a quiet way (*left*). (Magenta can play both warm and cool roles because the color includes both red and violet.)

• Neutral colors include grays, whites, and blacks. In the world of flowers, white conveys purity and elegance. In a formal black and white room (*opposite*), white lilies blend with the color scheme to preserve the air of sophistication.

Blue and red-violet flowers in a white room (left) *create a subtle focal point. White lilies* (opposite) *blend in, softening a room full of hard surfaces.*

Shaped to FIT

Although flower-arranging classes may introduce you to a vocabulary of formal shapes—round, triangular, fan, pyramid, vertical, and crescent—you need not follow a strict formula when you're arranging flowers for everyday enjoyment. A relaxed crescent (*left*) works well on a coffee table because it looks good from all sides. It's also low enough so people on the sofa can enjoy a whole-room view.

Round or loosely mounded bouquets are good choices for dining tables and coffee tables because they look good from all angles (*opposite*). Keep the display low so guests can see each other without peering through the flowers.

Horizontal arrangements typically arch from their center to form two mirror-image arms. Such arrangements work well on long, narrow tables and on mantels.

Because tulips lean toward the sunlight as it passes through windows, they are best suited for loose, relaxed arrangements (left). If you use polysilk tulips, gently shape the stems and petals to mimic the graceful quality of real ones.

Making ARRANGEMENTS

Once you decide on the basic shape for an arrangement, choose the floral stems. For arrangements with several flower types, select line materials, a focal flower, a secondary flower, and filler materials.

Line materials define the basic shape, height, and width of an arrangement. Pink astilbe defines the edges of a fruit-and-flower arrangement *(right)*. Peruvian lilies, peegee hydrangeas, and foliage are used in the bouquet *(opposite)*.

Focal flowers (lilies *right*, hydrangeas *opposite*) are the largest element in the arrangement. Insert them close to the rim of the vase, staying within the shape defined by your line materials.

Secondary materials (apples and crab apples *right*, yarrow *opposite*) transition between the line materials and the focal flowers and fill out the shape of the design. Filler materials (foliage or small flowers such as the chrysanthemums, *right*) do as their name suggests, filling in any holes so the arrangement looks balanced and complete.

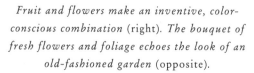

Fruit and flowers make an inventive, color-conscious combination (right). *The bouquet of fresh flowers and foliage echoes the look of an old-fashioned garden* (opposite).

Wide or NARROW?

L et the shape of your container guide the shape of your flower arrangement. A vase or pitcher that narrows at the neck makes easy work of arranging a loosely rounded bouquet of flowers such as hydrangeas *(left)*. Straight-stemmed flowers almost arrange themselves in this kind of container. For pleasing proportions, make the arrangement at least as tall as the vase and about twice as wide. Remember to strip all leaves from the stem below the waterline. This keeps the water cleaner, and in a clear glass vase, it looks tidier.

A widemouthed container lends itself to a full, fluffy bouquet of flowers such as goldenrod *(left)* or to a massive, rounded one *(opposite)*. You'll need many flowers to create a full mass. If you have an abundance of materials on hand, work from the outside in, crisscrossing stems inside the container to create a grid for holding the stems that need to stand upright. For a shortcut that will make arranging easier, fill the container with florist's foam and insert the stems where you want them.

A widemouthed pitcher holds an armload of goldenrod (left), *and hydrangeas practically arrange themselves in a narrow-neck one. A rustic maple syrup bucket suits the country look of assorted garden flowers and attractive weeds* (opposite).

Creative
CONTAINERS

Anything that holds water—or holds a watertight container—can serve as a vase. The container you choose has as much importance in the total design as the flowers themselves. Consider the color, texture, size, and shape of the materials you have to work with; factor in the location of the arrangement too. An assortment of clear glass vessels, from compotes to carafes, lets brightly colored cosmos and hydrangeas take center stage (*left*). The exclusive use of glass containers unifies the grouping; the variety of shapes and sizes keeps the look interesting.

Using antique urns and bowls for flower arrangements can reinforce room decor (*opposite*). To prevent water damage to valuable heirloom containers, reserve them for polysilk or dried arrangements. Piling fruit in a bowl is another way to bring color to the room without risking damage to the container. To pair flowers with the fruits, use polysilk stems or employ this trick: Buy florist's vials from a crafts store, fill each one with water, and insert a single stem through each rubber lid. Then nestle the vials down into the fruit.

Containers of various shapes can stand together when they're unified by color or material (left).

Using URNS

Urns work in any decor, and their classic shape gives them enduring appeal. Fill them with grass, balls of moss, or ivy for unexpected garden flavor inside the house. To grow grass in a cast-iron urn (*opposite*), fill the urn with potting soil and sprinkle on grass seed; keep the soil moist and wait. Seeds will take about 7 to 10 days to germinate.

Make your own moss-covered spheres (*below right*) in a few hours by gluing fresh sheet moss and different shades of reindeer moss to a plastic foam ball. Varying the size of the balls adds visual interest.

A 3-inch pot of English ivy slipped inside a 7-inch cast iron urn serves as the base for a photo display (*above right*). Use ready-made cardholders or garden markers to display your favorite black and white photos, inserting the stakes into the soil.

An ivy-filled urn shows off family photos with the help of wire photoholders (above right). Moss-covered spheres make a woodsy tabletop display (below right). The balls will stay green for a month or more if kept out of direct sunlight and spritzed occasionally with water. Copper plant markers can serve as place cards in tabletop patches of grass (opposite).

Unexpected PLACES

Give yourself and your whole household a treat: Place flowers in unexpected locations throughout your home. A bouquet in the bathroom (*opposite*) can give you the same lift as a long soak under a hot shower. A petite arrangement of your favorite flower at bedside or on the kitchen counter is like a little kiss, a gift to delight the senses. Make the laundry room more livable with pots of ferns and luxuriant houseplants. Place small garden bouquets in the sewing room or home office to lure yourself toward your workload. A shot of your favorite color can boost your mood: Look for it in unusual materials, such as grapes, clover, berries, and delphiniums (*left*) and give yourself a concentrated dose.

A petite pitcher is the starting point for a rhapsody in blue (left). What makes this arrangement fun is the use of unexpected materials: wild grapes, wild clover, and porcelain-berry vine. A big bouquet of flowers brings a romantic look to a bathroom (opposite).

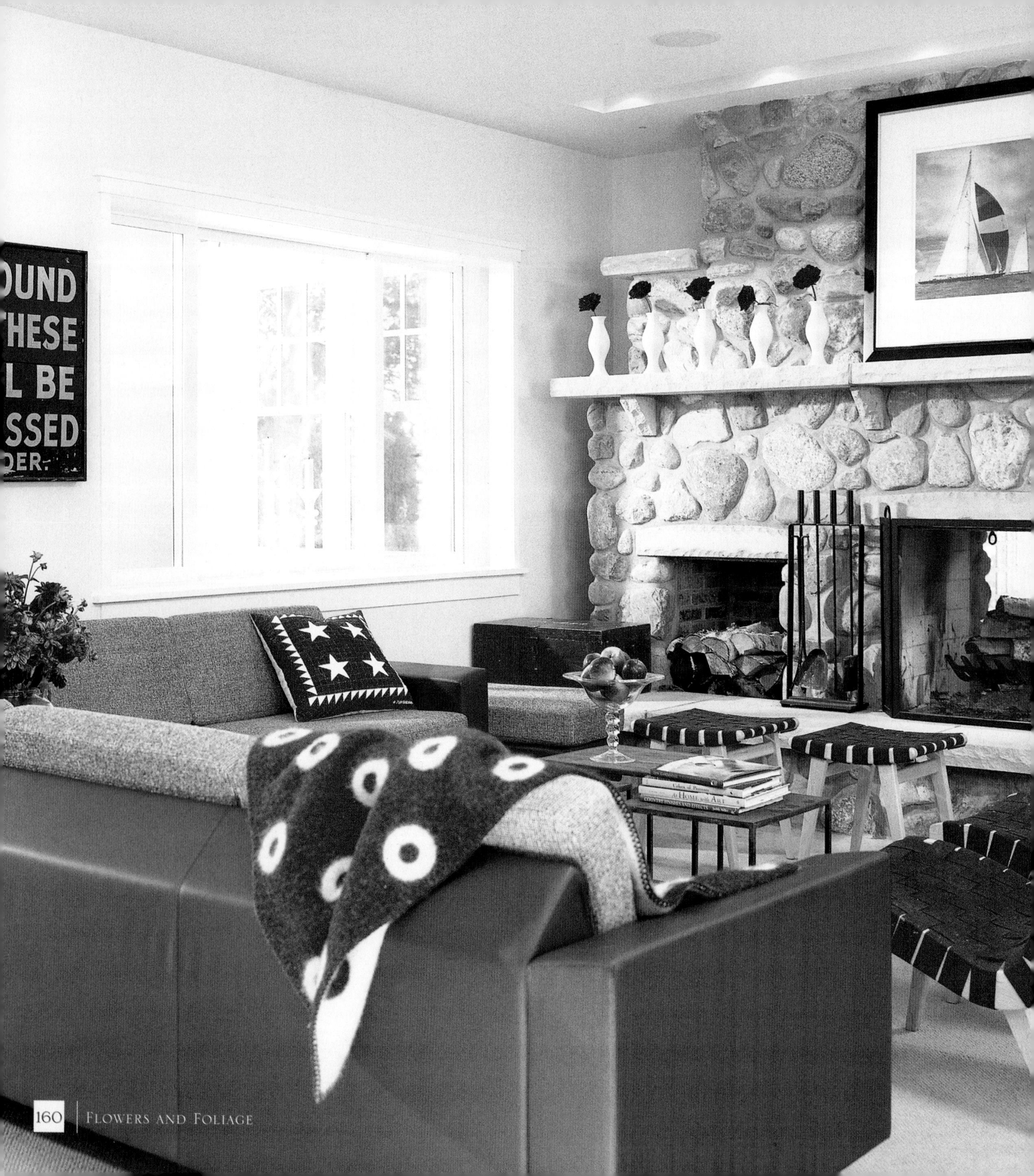
OUND
HESE
L BE
SSED
DER.

Simple STATEMENTS

Even when used in small doses, foliage and flowers can lift a room from lifeless to lively. To achieve this effect put the plants where they can have maximum impact—near the focal point of the room. A single ivy topiary on an entry table makes a formal, classic statement that reinforces the traditional style of the porcelain and other art objects (*left*). Single gerbera daisies in identical vases line up along the mantel (*opposite*) like a happy chorus line, bringing the modern spirit and bright color of the furnishings up to the fireplace wall. These examples prove that you don't have to invest in massive bouquets or forests of indoor plants to bring a feeling of the garden indoors. To achieve the best decorative effect, choose containers that harmonize with the style of your furnishings.

Gerbera daisies give the mantel a touch of happy color (opposite). *An ivy topiary and a moss-filled urn usher nature into a formal entry* (left).

Whether you use fresh garden flowers and potted plants or opt for their polysilk twins, change your floral displays regularly to give a room fresh style in an instant. Study these pages to see how easy it is to keep an indoor garden all year long.

Touch of Spring

In the spring let your garden be your guide. Fill glass vases with little glass gems—clear and bottle green—to help hold flower stems in place; then pop in daffodils and tiny grape hyacinths for a flowery affair. Delicate maidenhair fern in the tall urn adds softness. The rectangular tray, which normally catches keys and mail, can be used for a clean-lined display. Here it presents a compote and a martini glass filled with glass gems for sparkle and translucent color.

Tiers of Joy

"Easy-breezy" aptly describes this modest display. When you're short on time or your flower garden is fresh out of blooms, gather clippings of ferns and foliage to display in vases and mossy terra-cotta pots. Clear off the center of the chest to make way for a large tray, which will anchor the arrangement. A two-tiered tray is used here to showcase vases at different heights. To balance the lamp bring in a tall vertical element such as a group of books standing upright.

Oops a Daisy

Daisies make everyone smile, especially when they show up in unexpected places. "Plant" them in pots that repeat the white and yellow colors of the blooms; then add sprigs of ivy to soften the arrangement and visually tie the three pots together. What else unifies the look? You guessed it: the "elements of three" design rule. A single pot would look lonely on the surface of the chest, but three form a cozy, stable triangle that balances the other objects on display.

Run for the Roses

Instead of one big arrangement, make several small ones. Fewer than two dozen roses and about half a dozen tulips are all you need to re-create this artful arrangement. Set aside three groups of three or four roses each for the small arrangements. Mass the remaining flowers in the tallest vessel, using the graceful tulip stems to define the crescent shape and filling in with the roses. Use a variety of vases to loosen the formality and tradition associated with roses. Move the stack of books to the center to serve as a pedestal for one small bouquet.

Topiary Trio

When winter rolls around, spruce up your display with a mix of artificial and real topiaries planted in white French flower buckets. A white pitcher and a diminutive flower arrangement on the left balance the lamp and frames on the right. In front, a trio of candles on the rectangular tray gives warmth to the arrangement.

Centerpieces are synonymous with celebration. Celebrate every day with inexpensive floral centerpieces—homegrown, handpicked, and handsomely arranged by you. These lovely examples use flowers and foliage plucked from the garden and displayed in common containers from the kitchen.

Hydrangea Happiness

A footed glass compote serves as a vase for a lush hydrangea arrangement *(right)*. To ensure that the flowers and foliage stay in place, cut a piece of florist's foam to fit the bottom of the compote. Nestle the foam into a bed of glass gems to hide it. Bunch the hydrangeas in the center of the compote and push the stems into the foam. Fill in around the edges with smaller flowers, variegated foliage, and maidenhair fern. Elegant and easy, this arrangement lends formality and height to the table setting while still allowing guests to see each other across the table.

The More the Merrier

One floral arrangement dresses the table; a row of five bouquets turns a dinner into a party. Place the hydrangea arrangement in the center of the table. Then create several low, densely packed floral arrangements —ordinary chrysanthemums or carnations work well for this design—and add ferns or ivy for graceful lines that reach down toward the tabletop. (See "Hydrangea Happiness" for tips on keeping flowers in place.) For

Continued on page 167

variety fill compotes to overflowing with bunches of green grapes and sprigs of fern. End with a bang—that is, an explosion of color—by mixing pink and white roses, lilies, tulips, fern sprigs, and variegated ivy or other foliage into footed compotes. For extra sparkle lightly mist the arrangements right before dinner so that the water droplets on the leaves, petals, and grapes shine under the light.

Baskets of Bloom

Give flowers permission to leave the table—or at least the tabletop. For a special party flowers can decorate upholstered or slipcovered dining chairs (use flat-backed baskets to contain them against the chair backs). For each chair, gather a bunch of flowers and foliage, including at least one of the flower types in the centerpiece. Secure the stems in wet florist's foam and wrap the foam in a plastic bag. Place the arrangement in the basket, spreading the foliage to drape out of the basket. Using satin or organza ribbon, tie the ribbon around the chair back. (You may need to pin the ribbon to the chair's slipcover to help support the weight of the arrangement. This works best if the slipcover or upholstery is a sturdy fabric such as cotton duck. Silky or fine fabrics could be damaged by pins.) Hang the baskets on the back of each chair; or limit the display to the chairs at the opposite ends of the table.

L iving rooms need more than furniture; they need people to live in them. Without occupants, the space loses its purpose. Plants, strategically placed, can make the room feel more pleasant and inviting, drawing people in with their natural appeal.

Before

This living room is filled with an attractive mix of furniture, yet it lacks warmth and visual interest. Add flowers and foliage and voilà!—the room awakens and draws you into its intimate cottage garden theme. To achieve a similar look, follow these tips:

• Group vases of varying shapes and colors on a coffee table and fill them with contrasting flowers and foliage. Notice how the clean vertical lines of the irises contrast with the roundness of the geraniums. In any tabletop display, include a variety of heights to create an interesting path for the eye.

• If your room has large windows and your furniture is low, elevate the focal point of the room by adding tall plants. The potted palm beside the sofa fills the corner with greenery and draws the eye upward with its graceful arching fronds. Lined up on a tabletop behind the sofa, the topiaries lift the eye upward and make the room feel more spacious. Arranged in a stable triangle shape, they provide a dramatic and lively foreground to the wall of windows.

After

- Balance the tall elements in the room with plants placed on the floor. Greenery at armchair level (such as the ivy spilling out of the urn beside the chair) grounds your plantscape. Placing plants at different levels around the room creates a feeling of balance and helps lead the eye up and down through the space.

- For a decorative effect, cover the soil of potted plants with reindeer moss or other fresh moss (available from florists), or use dried moss from a crafts store. When you water the plants, the moisture will revive the moss too. If you prefer to use polysilk trees, tuck dried reindeer moss (available from crafts stores) around the base of the trunk for a woodland look. Grow your own pots of grass by sowing rye or wheat seed in a container of potting soil.

AMBIENCE

Decorate your entire home with an atmosphere of love.

For the most part, the art of accessorizing focuses on how a room looks. Accessories impact the room's appearance with their size, shape, color, and texture—features that please the eye. However, they also offer something less tangible, less visible: ambience—an atmosphere, a feeling. Think about the places where you have been the most comfortable, places that have become the backdrop for many of your happy memories. What smells and sounds were part of the experience? Do you recall the quality of light? With candles, accent lighting, and music, you can bring those fragrances, sounds, and light into your rooms to evoke the same sense of contentment, security, or delight.

A fragrant scent in the air, the intimate light from a candlescape, soothing music in the background—these subtle touches heighten home decorating. A room that indulges all the senses becomes welcoming and warm.

The right LIGHT

Two basic types of light influence the look and feel of your rooms. The first type—indirect light—illuminates the room in general without focusing on a specific object. Overhead and natural light are two sources of indirect lighting. (Indirect light is also called diffused or ambient light.)

Direct light, the second basic type, provides focused light. It can highlight an object (accent lighting) or provide illumination for a particular task (task lighting). Direct light draws your eye because it concentrates the illumination in one spot. Lamps, candles, sconces, and track lighting all provide direct light.

All rooms require both indirect and direct lighting. Watch how natural light settles on the walls and floor of your room and decide whether you need a supplemental artificial source for overall indirect lighting. Then consider the tasks that you'll perform in the space and add direct light accordingly. A lamp on a desk provides light for reading, while sconces wash the wall with light to create a special mood. Adding candles and decorative lamps around the room contributes to an inviting atmosphere.

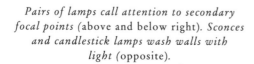

Pairs of lamps call attention to secondary focal points (above and below right). Sconces and candlestick lamps wash walls with light (opposite).

Made in the
SHADE

The right shade sets off a lamp the way a piece of jewelry sets off an outfit. How do you know which shade is best for your lamp? Think about lamps in terms of shape and style. On a traditional urn-shape lamp, (*opposite below*), the base is the dominant decorative element. A classic, tailored shade complements the style without competing with the urn. For a column, post, or candlestick base, however, let the shade make the decorative statement: Go all out with something frilly or floral to soften the look. If possible take along your lamp when you shop for a shade.

You'll also need to consider shade materials. Opaque shades focus light in one direction: down. Usually dark or bold in color, these shades add drama to a room. In living areas they pool light at seating level, making conversations cozy. In bedrooms they are ideal for reading lamps. Translucent shades provide diffused light that glows through the entire shade in every direction. White shades make light appear cool and clean; cream shades create a mellow glow. Translucent shades make a room feel casual and romantic.

Lamps work as stand-alone accessories or as part of a grouping. Use a stack of books to raise a lamp to the desired height in a table display (left and opposite above left).

The magic of
CANDLELIGHT

Long after the advent of electricity and lamplight, candles continue to charm.

Glowing candlelight has the power to elevate everyday activities into events. It can transform an ordinary room into an intimate retreat. Candlelight softens and soothes. It becomes a focal point but also draws the eye to the objects it illuminates.

Candles come in many shapes and sizes; the most common types are votives, tapers, pillars, and jar candles. Good quality candles contain highly refined food-grade wax combined with a high percentage of fragrance oil. Fine ingredients contribute to the longevity of a candle and and prevent excessive melting and smoke.

What constitutes a pleasant fragrance is a matter of personal opinion. Good-quality scented candles can engage the sense of smell—the sense most closely linked to memory and emotion.

Although white is always right for tapers, colorful ones can reinforce the room's color scheme (opposite). Dress up ordinary pillars with ribbon, taking care to keep the ribbon clear of the flame (left).

Creating
CANDLESCAPES

One flickering candle adds a warm glow to a room; a grouping of candles creates drama. Clustered candles have great allure. Groupings can also emphasize a particular decorating element, drawing your attention to a tabletop or shelf. A row of the same type of candle (all pillars, for example) is clean and uniform. A grouping of the same color candles reinforces dominant colors in a room. A collection of candles in different shapes, sizes, and colors supports a casual, informal decorating scheme.

When you group candles, let your imagination be your guide. Experiment with placement until the arrangement looks right. Center a large pillar candle and use it as your focal point, adding candles of different heights to build the display. Mix and match candle colors. Play with repetition by lining up one type of candle along a shelf. Or use scent as the common element; group candles according to fragrance, regardless of size or style.

Accessorizing with candles stretches your decorating dollar. For the greatest impact, mass candles, choosing a variety of heights and sizes (above and below left, opposite).

Clever
CONTAINERS

Candles gain clout when you display them in attractive containers. Think beyond candlesticks: How about platters, pedestals, or martini glasses? Mix and match containers to suit the setting. Some additional tips:

• Choose containers that complement the style of your space, either through contrasting colors or repeating shapes or motifs found elsewhere in the room. Plain white platters can suit any style, while chunky pottery looks best in a cottage- or country-style room.

• Create unity by grouping candleholders made of similar materials, such as crystal, iron, or silver.

• Add a twist: If you're grouping pillars on a platter, sprinkle the platter with confetti *(above left)*. In a dining room tweak a display of crystal candlestick holders by floating votives in water-filled martini glasses *(opposite)*. A compote filled with water can float several tiny flames *(below left)*.

For safety, always burn candles within sight (don't leave burning candles unattended). If you cluster candles, leave a sliver of space between them (above left).

Candle
CHARISMA

Candles are perhaps the most versatile of all accessories. They add style when displayed on pedestals and platters, when grouped together, and when used alone. Discover the extent of their adaptability: Display them in clever containers—ordinary household vessels that you have on hand. You'll be creating a one-of-a-kind display that reflects your personality.

Cups and saucers, whether china or crystal, and colored antique bottles make good candle containers. Candles also stand up well in glass vases, bowls, or jars *(above left)*; fill in around them with beans, rock salt, or even buttons *(see page 188)*. Fruit and vegetables can serve as containers too. Hollow out a hole large enough to hold the candle base. Tuck in leaves, twigs, or flowers to make a collar around the mouth of the opening; keep these materials clear of the flame *(opposite)*.

Combine a single pillar candle or a group of pillars with seasonal fruits and vegetables, dried or fresh, for an instant centerpiece (below left).

Specialty
CANDLES

Candles are more than a source of mood-setting light; they're decorative objects in their own right. Painted candles, liquid candles, candles with sand and potpourri mixed into the wax, and candles made of beeswax—these are only a few of the choices available.

Use specialty candles alone or in groupings. Most have specific care instructions; read the packaging and follow the directions for displaying and burning them.

All candles must be stored below 80 degrees F. Keep those with added ingredients such as leaves and glass pebbles at cooler temperatures to keep the objects encased in wax. Wrap painted candles in tissue paper to protect the paint. Store liquid candles upright.

One beeswax candle adds interesting texture to a grouping of traditional tapers (right). You can make your own painted candles using specialty paints available at crafts stores (opposite).

Decorating with lamps is an art. Deciding which light source to use where is a science. Different spaces require different kinds of illumination. The quantity of light and the way you distribute it determine how comfortable the room feels.

Lamplight

Begin with the right wattage. In rooms with televisions or in spaces where you want to relax, use 60-watt bulbs in uplights such as sconces and in lamps with translucent shades. For areas of activity, use 100 watts in downlights such as lamps with opaque shades, spotlights, and floor lamps. Keep in mind that one lamp generally illuminates 40 to 50 square feet.

Next, consider lamp placement.

- In living rooms and family rooms, overhead light is less welcoming than lamplight. Place a lamp beside or behind the sofa and each chair to accommodate reading in any location *(above right)*. To ensure a balanced distribution of light, position lamps to form a triangle. Lamps flanking the sofa need not be identical; however, aim to have the bottoms of the shades nearly even so they appear balanced. If needed, place a lamp on a stack of books so it matches the height of its counterpart.

- Accent lighting from candlestick lamps and picture lights *(right)* adds sparkle to a room. At night these little pools of light evoke warm and cozy feelings.

- A desk lamp sheds task light in a work area *(right)*. To maximize the illumination and reduce eyestrain, choose a lamp whose shade is at seated eye level, about 15 inches from the work surface. An opaque shade forces all the light down toward your desk. However, a white or cream-color translucent shade is a better choice if the lamp has to illuminate both the room and the desk.

- Sconces are often chosen for their looks, yet they can be a practical source of light as well. They provide ambient uplight—indirect illumination that is adequate for such pass-through areas as halls and foyers.

C andles are one of the most evocative decorating tools. Their shape, color, and texture appeal to the eye and enhance any decorating scheme. When lit, candles provide soft, romantic light; fragrance comes into play when you use scented candles. Tap into the power of fragrance to create a welcoming and comfortable ambience in your home.

Candle Fragrance

- A room that smells good to you will make you feel good too. Some candles release their scent even before you light them. In most cases, however, burning releases the fragrance, which lingers in the room after you've doused the flame.

- Science explains the power of scent: One of the fastest routes to the part of the brain that controls your sense of well-being is through the 25,000 odor receptors in the nose. It's harder to explain fragrance preferences; they are highly personal, so only you (and other household members) can decide which ones create the atmosphere that's most comfortable for you.

- Some herbal fragrances are believed to have therapeutic value. Lavender, for example, is said to encourage relaxation, so lavender candles are a good choice for bedrooms—or for bathrooms if you like to take long, relaxing soaks in the tub. Rosemary and sage stimulate beta waves in the brain, making you feel more alert; a rosemary-scented candle on your desk may give you the energy to pay bills.

- Non-herbal fragrances include florals and spice-based scents. Florals such as peony, rose, and gardenia can transport you to your grandmother's garden. Vanilla-scented candles smell good without suggesting specific cooking associations, while cinnamon-apple candles evoke home and holidays.

- Choose one fragrance to create an overall mood in your home. Use this scent in the entry and throughout the main living areas. If your bedroom and bath are set well apart from the main areas, they can host a second fragrance. If you notice the two scents competing, eliminate the second one.

- For safety, always burn candles within sight. Keep overhanging flowers, fabric, and all flammable materials clear of flames. Before lighting a new wick, trim it to about $1/4$ inch. Each time you light a candle, rotate the candle one-quarter turn and trim the wick to $1/4$ inch above the surface of the wax. As the candle burns, keep the pool of melted wax free of wick trimmings, matches, or other debris.

- Allow pillar candles to burn one hour for each inch of diameter. For example, a 3-inch candle should burn three hours (but no more than three). Wax has "memory"—allow the molten wax pool to reach the maximum width (about $1/8$ inch to $1/4$ inch from the edge of the candle) and it will continue to burn to that width for the life of the candle. To preserve the integrity of the outer shell, gently mold the outer edges of the wax while the wax is still warm.

Index

Giving Back   A legacy of helping others

by Christi Carter Urschel
*Founder, Home Interiors
Charitable Foundation*

*Mary Crowley founded the
legacy of giving in 1957.*

Home Interiors, the
company founded by
my grandmother, Mary
Crowley, has its very roots
in the idea of offering
women a means of making
better lives for themselves
and their families. She
believed passionately that
our homes are a haven, with
the power to nurture loving
relationships. That spirit
lives today in the Home
Interiors commitment to the
Women Build program of
Habitat for Humanity.

DECORATING LIVES
For more than 45 years,
Home Interiors has been
empowering women to
improve their own lives by
helping other women. Now
100,000 strong, our

decorating consultants across
the United States, Puerto
Rico, Canada, and Mexico
help others make their
homes into havens through
the artful arrangement of
accessories and accent
furniture. Home Interiors is
the largest direct seller of
home decor products in
North America. We are
especially proud of our new
partnership with Meredith
Corporation, publisher of
Better Homes and Gardens®

books and magazines. Home
Interiors and Gifts is currently
marketing a new line of fine
home decor products under the
Better Homes and Gardens
brand, which will result in new
collections of products that
reflect the great style of this
beloved brand.

A SPIRIT OF GIVING
Although Mary Crowley had a
history of supporting causes and
philanthropies that shared her

values, the Home Interiors
Charitable Foundation was not
formally organized until the
tragic events of September 11,
2001. Wanting to help, the Home
Interiors decorating consultants
prompted the company to
develop products that could be
sold for the direct benefit of the
9/11 victims and their families.
Within a few weeks, the women
had raised $1 million for the
American Red Cross's Liberty
Disaster Fund.

*Christi Carter (fourth from the left, standing) and Home Interiors volunteers
at the Long Beach, California, Blitz Build site. These dedicated sales
associates put in hours of building time and sold a special Home Interiors
Habitat for Humanity candle to raise money to eliminate poverty housing.*

Giving Back

The Women Build program empowers women with the necessary skills and training to build a home from start to finish. Since 1991, women crews have built more than 350 Habitat houses in the United States.

Home Interiors Women Build volunteers lift a roof truss onto a Habitat for Humanity house. Through building homes with Habitat for Humanity, the organization helps others find comfort in safe and affordable housing.

The build site of a Dallas house that Home Interiors built through Habitat for Humanity's Women Build program. Through houses like these, the vision of the partnership between Home Interiors and Habitat for Humanity is growing stronger.

A NEW PARTNERSHIP

In 2003, the Home Interiors Charitable Foundation reached a turning point and began focusing efforts toward Habitat for Humanity International, specifically its Women Build initiative. The Women Build program brings women volunteers together to continue the mission of Habitat for Humanity—to build simple, decent, affordable houses in partnership with those who lack adequate shelter. Since 1976, Habitat has built more than 50,000 houses with families throughout the United States and another 100,000-plus houses in communities around the world.

RAISING THE ROOF

Home Interiors and Women Build make perfect partners because each is dedicated to recognizing and acknowledging the value and dignity of women. Women Build promotes the involvement of women in the construction of Habitat houses, and as these photos attest, hundreds of Home Interiors volunteers have pitched in. The projects provide an opportunity for women to learn construction skills in a supportive environment. The initiative also addresses the impact of substandard housing on the health and well-being of children.

A LEGACY OF HOPE

My grandmother's life has had a profound influence on everyone around her. Her belief in the goodness of people and her desire to inspire in others the hope and optimism that came naturally to her left a legacy of giving that will long endure. Over the years, Home Interiors has given more than $70 million to charitable causes and community organizations. That legacy continues through the labor of love that has become this book. All of my proceeds from its sales will be donated to Women Build at Habitat for Humanity.